GET M.O.V.E.D

GET

M.O.V.E.D.

Mapping Out Victory Each Day

DEANA WILLIAMS

Please feel free to reach out to me via my website/blog: www.getmoved.org. This book may be purchased for educational, spiritual, business or personal use.

Disclaimer and limit of liability: Please be advised that the information in this book will affect people in many different ways. It can be a vital tool and should be used as a resource to map out victory each day. It is not intended to replace medicines, discredit diagnosis or replace professional services when medically necessary. This book can be used in conjunction with or as a supplemental tool to go from bad to good or from good to great!

As "YOURLIFECOACHDEANA" and founder of Taking My Life Back Empowerment Conferences, it is my sincere prayer that this book sets the foundation as God blesses you to start and complete this journey to your "divine destiny". Everything God has for you will be for you!

Edited by: Randall Horton

Book cover and interior layout design: Analer Digital Media

ISBN: 978-0-9972833-4-1

ISBN: (ebook) 978-0-9972833-1-0

Scripture Quotations from the KJV

Definitions are from Webster's Dictionary

Website/blog: www.getmoved.org

Facebook: https://www.facebook.com/deana.williams.1800

Email: devinepurposeorg@yahoo.com

CONTENTS

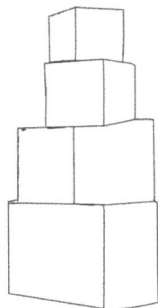

FOREWORD

Get M.O.V.E.D
(Mapping Out Victory Each Day)

Get M.O.V.E.D (Mapping Out Victory Each Day) is an extraordinary and exhilarating guide that takes us on a journey to the top of our spiritual mountain. If you have plateaued or feel stuck where you are in Life, Deana Williams invites you to climb to higher heights through daily devotions and insightful activities. These exercises are for anyone searching for a new way to transform each obstacle in Life into an opportunity to grow spiritually.

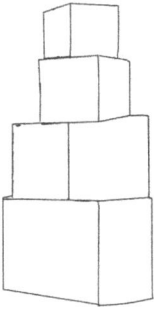

Get M.O.V.E.D. will motivate you each day to become victorious in your personal and professional life. You will be inspired to change how you see yourself, family, friends, co-workers and community. You will also learn to live with passion and on purpose. You will never accept defeat and find victory each day.

The next 12 weeks of your life will be filled with adventure, adversity and awareness as Deana's guide teaches you how to live and not simply exist.

Warm regards,

Malik

I. Malik Saafir, President & Founder
Janus Institute For Justice
Educate. Engage. Empower!

DEDICATION

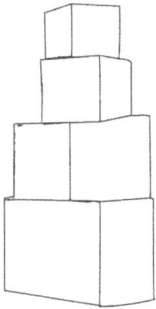

This book is dedicated to my daughter, Kaitlyn; my nieces, Taylor, Joniya, Jonesha, Raven, and Jersei; and my nephews: Clarence, Terrance, Trevion, DeVonte, Michael, Trevius, B.J, Jamychael and Javion. May your dreams extend beyond your horizons!

This book is also dedicated to my family and friends, immediate and extended! Lastly, in memory of my parents, "Radio" James and Delores "Sug" Williams, eternally treasured!

INTRODUCTION

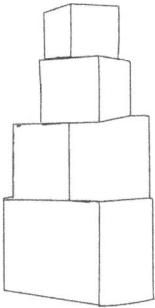

The purpose of this book is to get you M.O.V.E.D! Mapping Out Victory Each Day will be your mission. This book will serve as a blueprint and guide, and most importantly, a map into a better future. The tasks will be doable and not too time consuming. This book is for the young, old, lost, seeking, male, female, recently found, any race and the newly awaken. This book will enlighten you beyond measure and equip you beyond superficial needs and/or wants. This book will serve as a solid foundation for your new level of living. This book will help you map victories over the next 90 days. This book will evolve around you. It will cause you to cease existing and activate conscious living daily. You will experience self-empowerment through self-discovery. Your life will never be the same because you will never be the same. Over the next 90 days you will embark on a journey that will take you through three phases. You will be asked to identify, recall and reflect to create building blocks or stepping-stones for your new level of living.

Honesty will be the key to your overall success. Know that success is where opportunity and preparation meet. Be prepared for this amazing opportunity to become empowered. You will be catapulted to new horizons and boundaries will be expanded. This book will reflect a season; 12 journeys (weeks)/3 phases or 90 days; whichever makes you feel comfortable. The reason why I reference this journey as a season is because the Bible says to everything there is a *Season*. In other words, I need you to understand your now is not forever, only a season. When you look at Season, know that each season represents a distinct period of time and reflects a certain status, however, change is on the way and inevitable. This book will cause you to reflect, realize, remember, recognize, reminisce, relate and re-engage. You will have to actively participate and be engaged.

Although seasons are referenced, you will have daily tasks, creating new habits and perspectives. By participating daily you will move forward and your past will cease to exist. This book requires you to become the standard by which you will start to live. It will also cause you to start requiring more from others as well as yourself. You will benefit you wholeheartedly. Through readings and daily assignments, you will build and set a firm foundation for your best life yet.

In each phase, I will share some of my personal experiences to get you set out on each journey. It will serve as your personal guide to set you on the right path. Therefore, day one of each journey will require a few more minutes, as it will include reading and an activity. I hope my stories enlighten, uplift and encourage you.

Please, I repeat, please refrain from sympathizing or empathizing with me, as I am a Victor no longer a victim!

In journeys 1-4, you will dig deep within and uncover things that caused your current or recent state of being. You must be open and honest. Some days you will ponder, wonder, laugh and/or cry but all will be essential in your growth. You will experience some pain but the reward will be your greatest gain.

In journeys 5-8, you will transition, becoming the creator and author of your next chapters. You will be M.OV.E.D. to an empowered state of being. This is when you will begin to live! The level on which you will begin to live will be on a whole new level. You will charter unfamiliar territory. Each day will work in your favor thus creating a new and better you. You will no longer accept what has been issued or given. Instead, you will start making decisions that re-define you and represent what you deserve.

In journeys 9-12, you will be set up to succeed. You will recognize your purpose. You will apply what you know and have learned. Your purpose will be revealed and it alone will catapult you to higher living. Your passions will be ignited and the fire will begin to burn deep within. In other words, you will be M.O.V.E.D. to live your best life now!!!!

Note: This is an active process and requires your full attention! You will be asked to do things and you will need a few supplies. Some supplies may include: pencils, pens, glue, scissors, pictures, magazines, etc. So, your first day will possibly be your longest day of each journey.

Think on this...

Why did I say "Get M.O.V.E.D?" I am basically charging you to map out victories in your life on a daily basis. "Get" just signifies putting things into motion. As this journey concludes, you will have addressed yourself mentally, emotionally, physically, spiritually, religiously, in other words holistically! Remember that this journey is YOUR journey. This journey is about you and most importantly, for YOU! You will realize, prioritize and visualize. Your life will take on new meaning and direction. Lastly, you will move into your next season!

For I know the thoughts that I think toward you, saith the Lord, thoughts of peace, and not of evil, to give you an expected end.

Jeremiah 29:11 (KJV)

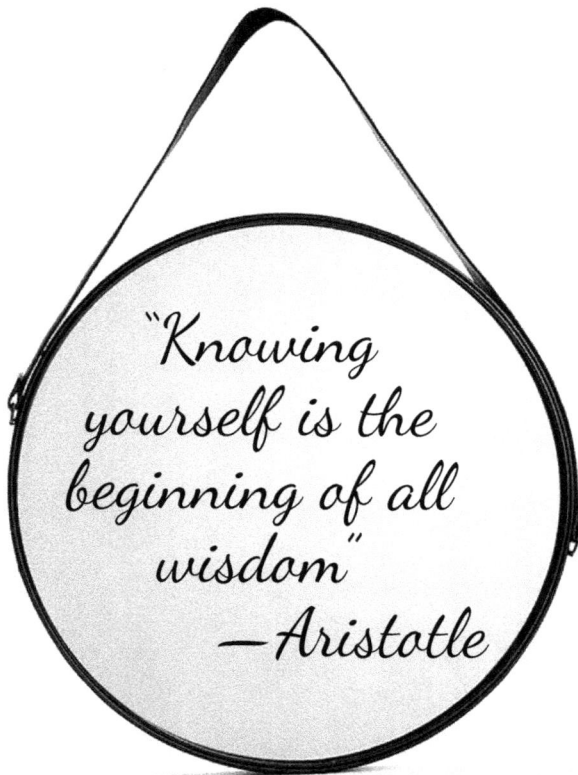

"Knowing yourself is the beginning of all wisdom"
—Aristotle

PRE M.O.V.E.D SURVEY

Before you begin, you need to do a brief "Pre-M.O.V.E.D." survey, indicating your current status:

Take a few minutes to complete this brief survey; it should be 5 minutes or less.

Current status: Single, Married, Widowed, Divorced, etc._____

Current Age: _____

Current Personal Goal: _____

_____

Current Professional Goal: _____

_____

Current Financial Stance: Broke, Making it, Stable, Planning, Don't know, Could be better, etc. _____

Current Purpose: Self, Group, Work, Church, etc.

_____

_____

Goal: What do you hope to gain from this book? _____

_____

_____

_____

_____

_____

To everything there is a season, and a time to every purpose under the heaven: A time to be born, and a time to die; a time to plant, and a time to pluck up that which is planted; A time to kill, and a time to heal; a time to break down, and a time to build up; A time to weep, and a time to laugh; a time to mourn, and a time to dance; A time to cast away stones, and a time to gather stones together; a time to embrace, and a time to refrain from embracing; A time to get, and a time to lose; a time to keep, and a time to cast away; A time to rend, and a time to sew; a time to keep silence, and a time to speak; A time to love and a time to hate; a time of war, and a time of peace.

Ecclesiastes 3:1-8 (KJV)

Losing, Identifying and Finding Self

Journey 1/Day 1

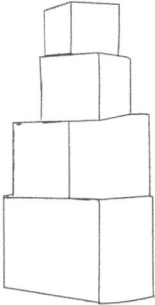

I am the second of six, the one who is always "so-n-so's" little/big sister, the one always-seeking individuality; yet, still pleased with simply being known. As a young child, life was good! We had a pony when others were wishing for a bike. Wanting and getting any and everything was a way of life for us, we didn't know any other way. My dad spoiled us rotten. My mom was the disciplinarian and boy was she! We all knew not to test her. I can't ever recall her spanking us but if you ask one of my siblings they would beg to differ. In my mind, life was just the way it was supposed to be, good. My dad was known by all and his statue was ever-present in our community. He was known as "Radio James" and we just had to mention his name. Some would say we were born with certain rites of passages being "Radio's kids." I was a professional at calling his name: Radio. I took it to another level, I'm sure. I still hear stories about when I was little and/or when "Radio James" was alive. My dad was someone special to so many people, not just his children.

We lived our lives daily with no thought of change, which was a big mistake. Most would say we took life for granted. Little did we know our lives would forever be changed on April 11, 1977 (Easter). My mom was accidently shot. My mom died. She always kept a .22 caliber pistol with her. But the safety failed when she laid her gun down, and it went off. Her life was over at the tender age of 28. I was only 7, my oldest sister 8 and my youngest sister 1. My parents were raising two other girls and the oldest girl; Thedora was the one who told us what happened. I didn't believe her so she got my momma's bra out of the laundry basket and showed us the blood-stained bra. As the news spread, people showed up in droves at times to talk with my dad. Some came to get what "Sug," my Mom, would have wanted them to have. I remember sitting on the bed as everyone came and took what they wanted, never lending care or concern to the 6 motherless children left behind. My dad didn't say a word; he just said that's how people are. Now our lives would be forever changed. The families of the two girls came and got them. Everyone had advice for my dad but he didn't listen, he did what he had to do. He raised us as a single father.

Did I forget to mention, my dad was 37 years older than my mom? He was 65 with 6 young children, ages 1-8. What a job, what a Man! In the next year our childhood home burned down and we had to move to one of my dad's rental properties. It was where some of his workers lived, nothing like our home. My Dad did everything to make sure we wanted for nothing and over-compensated in every way to make sure we didn't lack anything. Some would even say we were spoiled. That was okay. We were allowed to be spoiled because we were "Radio James' kids" and no one would say anything even if they wanted to. Life seemed great as it could be but, really, that was only perception.

Five years passed and our lives would change once again. A young man entered our home, robbed and killed our daddy. Life as we knew it was gone and we were at the mercy and hand of others. I think I read we were deemed orphans and wards of the court. In other words, we were now lost and in the hands of others. The years to come were anything but certain and our way was blind. The life I knew was gone; the identity I knew was gone. I had questions but no answers. My new road was fast approaching to becoming a troubled child. I was full of hurt, anger and resentment. I didn't know who to be mad at and I couldn't trust anyone. All I did know was that this thing called "life" was over-rated!

Losing, Identifying and Finding Self

There was no joy in my soul. My siblings and I were taken in, put out, moved around and eventually split up. I remember being called a gypsy. I had simply lost my identity and had no clue who I was or who I was supposed to become. Eventually, I ended up in college after enduring abuse at various levels, including rape, incest and molestation. I had even managed to have a boyfriend. You know "the one" and it was, for me, a good thing. Then time eventually separated us. We talked and wrote like nobody's business but infidelity brought those walls down. Never again, would this happen. I gave myself time, you know, time where you are supposed to be soul searching and recreating yourself, yeah right. My sister ran across the next good man and introduced us. Why not, I asked myself? What did I have to lose; it was only one date that lasted for six years. If only I had allowed myself to wake up and not accept what was not to be. I accepted a plan that someone else had planned for their life, and I thought it would work for me, so I adopted it. He was not a part of my plan, but I became confused and believed I had to accept love right then and there. So I gave it my all, head first, body second and heart later. Then he let me down, he cheated. I only wanted to love and be loved, unconditionally that is. I didn't understand, I did what had to be done, accepted him, whether I wanted to or not. I didn't love myself therefore, I couldn't love him. I had absorbed his personality. I was true to what he stood for. He had been dating his "mini-self." Hell, he should have been happy; he had the best situation possible. My selflessness even over shadowed his selfishness. Eventually, he showed his true colors when I caught him cheating. I doubted myself, and what I knew to be true. I left the scene allowing him opportunity to make me doubt myself. He made me believe that I didn't know what I really knew. This was truly a bad place to be. Ultimately, I didn't know me and was lost without a clue of self. After the relationship ended, I spent years soul-searching, trying to make his wrong right. I realized I had absorbed his personality. Love was present but had not been the driving force in our relationship. In fact, I exuded selflessness instead of identity in this relationship, thus becoming lost more so than before. No more. Walls went up, I had to protect myself, I didn't trust myself to find my destiny. Simply, I was lost and had no identity and no direction, but I now realized it. Discoveries are great, if you are open to newness and change!

So, I first want to commend you for taking this step to change your life. I want you to know you are not alone, this happens daily to people. Although your story might be different from my story, we end up on the same road, lost without a clue. It's not about being lost, it's about staying lost. This is your chance to pick a path and go with intentions in that direction. You deserve it! Appreciate your past but enjoy your new journey. You will travel uncharted territory and reach higher heights. Your destination will be great and your life will be fulfilling. Your future will be designed by your actions and will not happen accidentally. You will find your "self," thus discovering your purpose! Your next season is on the way!

Oftentimes we focus on other people, things and somehow lose ourselves. We sometimes lose sight of what is and what should be important. We tend to give to everyone while neglecting self for the sake of right and what we believe is love. We, in short, absorb the personality of others and our identity becomes compromised until we rectify self and learn to put "self" in its rightful place, NOW!

Losing, Identifying and Finding Self

Self-Assessment
Journey: Know Thyself

Welcome to this week's journey where you will complete a short and sweet self-assessment. This will be important because you must know yourself before you can begin to know anyone else or anything else. Self is key and fundamental. Knowing self means you know your values, your worth and most importantly, your purpose. We have a blueprint to our identity and what it takes to make us, us! Self is the pure essence of who you are and what you stand for. So many people desire to know themselves but in life tend to lose themselves within the people and world around them.

So, this is not an all-inclusive or a one shot deal but an indefinite ever-evolving basic foundation for moving forward in life. Try to answer the following questions honestly and to the best of your ability. If you know the answers without deep thought, great! If not, that's ok too, considering this a pivotal turning point in your life. The best is yet to come! By the end of the book you will know yourself better than before, and more importantly, better than anyone else.

Name: (Research the meaning of your name.) _____

Favorite color: _____

Favorite flower: _____

Favorite song/artist: _____

Favorite book/author: _____

Favorite past time: _____

Favorite scripture: _____

Favorite hobby: _____

Favorite quote: _____

Favorite joke: (We should all be able to laugh.) _____

_____

Do you have a bucket list? _____ If so, What's on it?: _____

Journey 1/Day 1

Losing, Identifying and Finding Self

Assessment is when you evaluate or give an appraisal. An assessment can be internally or externally driven. There are usually reasons one takes part in an assessment. An assessment can bring you validation, confirmation or need for separation. I am not sure why you are here but there must be a reason. Chances are a season is over or you are on the horizon of a new season in your life, personally or professionally. Regardless of what the "Who, what, when, where and why," I am excited that you are here. Today, I ask that you do a brief assessment of you and your life in general.

If you have done this before, proceed as follows. If not, just do your best.

Write about a time when you did a self-assessment. What brought you to that point? Chances are a need for CHANGE. Did you take heed or just overlook the obvious? If you haven't, take time to do a brief assessment now. You can ask a few friends or family members for references but be careful; you can't ask a crook to be honest. Don't put yourself in the way of the enemy to be attacked. I really want you to be able to answer for self, after all, that is the sole purpose of this journey. How did your assessment differ from theirs? Who was on point? Be honest.

_____

_____

_____

_____

_____

_____

_____

_____

_____

_____

_____

_____

_____

Losing, Identifying and Finding Self

After the last activity, the assessment exercise, how do you feel? Write about it, this is necessary for growth.

_____

_____

_____

_____

_____

_____

_____

_____

_____

_____

_____

_____

_____

_____

_____

_____

_____

_____

_____

_____

_____

_____

_____

_____

Journey 1/Day 3
Losing, Identifying and Finding Self

Find your favorite scripture or quote that talks about self, character or integrity. Write it here, and then write about why it's your favorite. Describe how it motivates or empowers you. You may have more than one, feel free to reflect on a few if you would like. Once you have completed this task, take five minutes to reflect on the key words. Recite at least one of your scriptures or quotes as a daily affirmation. For example, one of my favorite scriptures simply says that I am wondrously made.

_____

_____

_____

_____

_____

_____

_____

_____

_____

_____

_____

_____

_____

_____

_____

_____

_____

_____

_____

Journey 1/Day 4
Losing, Identifying and Finding Self

Visualize then draw or paste magazine images here that remind you of your character. Keep in mind that you must be honest. Draw an alligator snout if you talk too much, a big nose if you are nosey, a snake if you are a sneaky, an elephant if you have a great memory, a dog if you are an protector, a lion if you rule, a halo if you are an angel, etc.

Journey 1/Day 5
Losing, Identifying and Finding Self

Go out and do something you enjoy. Go out and do one of your favorite things by yourself, remember this is about you. You must spend time by yourself in order to know thy self. Note: whatever you choose to do can be simple but it must be for you. Be sure to research free things in your community, you would be surprised! Go window-shopping, buy yourself flowers, drive through the neighborhood you hope to live in. Open houses are great or go test-drive your dream car! Watch a live sporting event, go to a wine tasting or take a long country drive. Have fun! What did you do? Write about it here.

_____

_____

_____

_____

_____

_____

_____

_____

_____

_____

_____

_____

_____

_____

_____

_____

_____

_____

Journey 1/Day 6
Losing, Identifying and Finding Self

In order to grow you must leave your comfort zone. Go out and do something that frightens you or something you have been fearful of. In other words step outside the box. Go out to a new place, strike up a conversation with a stranger, ask someone out that you have been admiring from afar. (The choice is yours; it could be exercising, changing your makeup, getting a new haircut/style, growing a beard etc. It can be anything you have longed to do but never had the courage to do.) The important thing to remember here is that it must be done. Write your challenge here, once you have completed it, write about the experience, give details. It may be a small challenge, don't worry; we are just getting started. By the end of this season, you will be more than a conqueror!

_____

_____

_____

_____

_____

_____

_____

_____

_____

_____

_____

_____

_____

_____

_____

_____

_____

_____

Journey 1/Day 7
Losing, Identifying and Finding Self

Reflection: How did it go this week? What worked, what didn't, and how did it all feel? Remember to journal, your past experiences will afford your new future.

_____

_____

_____

_____

_____

_____

_____

_____

_____

_____

_____

_____

_____

_____

_____

_____

_____

_____

_____

_____

_____

_____

_____

Getting to Know Self beyond the Surface

Journey 2/Day 1

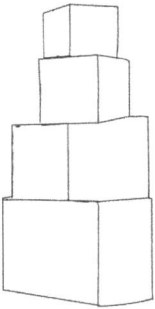

A parentless child who had not asked to be born was now solely at the hands of others. As an orphan of the court, I felt as though I had been wronged in various ways. Why did my parents have to die? Why were my siblings and I left behind? Being young in mind and heart without a true understanding of who is in control, everything gets discombobulated. I eventually developed an indirect resentment towards God but didn't really know that to be so. I say indirect because I was hurt and angry and blamed people for all that was wrong when really God was in control. Now, that was hard to understand and be real about. How and why plagued my thoughts with no answers in sight. My actions spoke louder than my words. Don't get me wrong, I would never speak out against God. I had always believed in God but something was wrong. I didn't know this for a very long time, in fact, I had no clue. I just traveled with my feelings on my sleeves and my heart in my hand. Also growing up in church with other people's belief and ways, I would dare not say it. I was very sad and cried often. I was looking for love in all the wrong places and I became promiscuous, allowed myself to be used and abused and allowed myself to believe or accept this as love. In other words, justifying and validating the wrongdoings of others became a common thread for me. Everyone else mattered and I had a pseudo sense of worth. Eventually, envy and jealousy consumed me and the "whys" bombarded me in a major way. I became a sad story and a sad song. No laughter in my heart and no joy in my spirit.

Don't get me wrong, I learned to mask my pain with a smile but my heart was heavy and sad.

Anytime I could get a good cry in I would. I had no self-worth, no sense of self-value and at times believe what I was told. I was not the first and not the last to go through some things but I certainly felt alone. There were things I carried in secret for years because I was ashamed and didn't want to be judged. I was my worst critic and started to feel like I deserved some of what happened to me, even though I now know differently. Love was supposed to be a great thing but love hurt in so many ways. I was taught at an early age to stay away from strangers because they would hurt me. No one ever said to watch out for the ones that are close to you; boy was I in for a rude awakening. Not knowing that I would survive and that these things would pass, I certainly worried and stressed for many years. Sleepless nights and cloudy days became a norm for me. I didn't know that my life was supposed to be different. I remember walking to class and crying when no one else was around, drying my tears as soon as someone moved into sight. I would go home to my hometown church on weekends and "testify," and by the time I finished, it seemed as if everyone else was crying with me. The Pastor would always say, "Just pray about it daughter." I kept asking him to tell me what "it" was. I could then pray it away. Years passed and so did "it," eventually. I begin to sing a little, laugh a little and one day realized that "it" was no longer a stronghold in my life. I even found what I thought was love. To my dismay, my past was still dictating my present and future. History repeated itself, I begin to allow someone else dreams to matter more than mine, I even became the wind beneath their wings while I was gasping for air. Suffocation by any means leads to death, be it a dream, goal, aspiration, fire, light, life, air or you.

Then God allowed things to go south. He put me by myself so I could get to know Him and myself. I was in a new, strange and unfamiliar place. What now? Where now? How? When did my sense of self begin to develop? I had to get to know me and what I stood for and what I believed in. I even realized what "it" was. It had been my frustration with life and how things had happened. How did God allow these things to happen, didn't He love me? Then I realized, He did indeed love me. He is not a respecter of person and it rains on the just as well as the unjust. In other words, He allowed but He never left nor did he forsake me. Even through my trials and tribulations, my triumphs would reign. So, I began to know myself on a deeper level. I began to build a foundation. I made sure I had pillars of strength to uphold my beliefs and ways of life. I began to make decisions for my tomorrows not just today. I even planned for the future and knew my actions played a great part in the outcome. I even began to journal with rules not to look back for certain periods of time; this allowed me to see my growth. It was not always pleasant or pretty but it was growth. All of sudden, I didn't accept what people offered or gestured, instead I had ideas about how I should and would be treated. Goals and dreams became a part of me. This week, I ask that you do a deeper self-analysis. This time you will do an analogy, comparing self to an animal, color, fruit and flower. This will bring out the qualities that you exemplify daily. Sometimes when comparing one thing to another, it's easier to see relevance or irrelevance. It becomes clearer what stands out or what should not stand out. The topics mentioned above are just suggestions and are not the only things you can use. Just know why you chose what you chose and be able to expand. It simply highlights the qualities of your character, integrity and identity. In essence it is a snapshot or portrait of you. These things show up daily in your character and personality. They are validated daily with people on a daily basis.

I was awakened to myself and my life. I no longer was able to dwell in darkness; instead I was forced to move toward the light. I not only moved toward the light but I desired light. I wanted to be seen and heard; most importantly, I knew God loved me. I also started to know that God was working in, on and through me. All my life, the balance of me had depended on what other people deposited into me and my spirit, no more. I began to build up my self-worth-bank and the value of my balance was priceless.

One of the best things you can do is to equate yourself with something tangible. Tangible means that you can touch it; it is real and can be treated as fact. For this next journey, we will reference our checking account. How many people are depositing into your account? How many people are withdrawing from your account? Is your account overdrawn? Do you keep good accounting records or do you carelessly spend? Maybe I should back track. Do you have a freestanding account or is someone else the keeper of you and your life? Can you mange wisely and effectively or do you carelessly act now and hope for the best later? Do you have a balance to cover what has to be covered? Are you mindful of your time and spending? If not, take time to establish your account, reconcile and budget your account. You can't afford overdraft fees, the cost is too great!

Journey 2/Day 1
Getting to Know Self Beyond the Surface

How did you do in Journey 1? Did you know the answers in week 1? Did you have to ask somebody? Be honest! This next week I ask you to go beyond the shallow surfaces. In this next assignment you have to correlate your answers to match your personality/character/demeanor. This will take a little more time because this needs to reflect you, not someone else's opinion of you. I ask you to venture in your imagination and give the best answer possible... dig deep, think big.

This assignment will cause you to tell the truth. Are you good, bad or indifferent? If you can do this, you will better understand yourself, as well as others around you. You will have insight on various levels, whether it's work or play. This will really benefit you in friendship, relationships, both personally and professionally.

This assignment will tell you if you are shy, bold, outspoken, an introvert, an extrovert, an altruist, or a narcissist. In a nutshell, welcome to your identity. Here are a few examples to get you started, choose one that will get you to the next assignment.

(Pick any animal; bird, cat, dog, fish, rabbit, lion, cheetah, tiger, elephant, stallion, etc)

If I were an animal, I would be an eagle because I can soar to the top; however, I can survive at the bottom. My gift of discernment is like an eagle's vision: keen and attentive to detail. As wide as the eagle's wings spread, I find myself very protective of those that I love. My greatest survival skill, much like that of an eagle, is that I can and will always rise above my greatest adversaries.

If I were a fruit, I would be a banana, because just like a banana, I can be good for you or like the peel, I can be hazardous to your health. One color represents that what you see is what you get. The true me remains the same even after the outer layer has been peeled away. Plainly put, I am simple yet complex, the same no matter what.

If I were a color, I would be a blue. Blue comes in various shades, whether it be for power, royalty, or peace. No matter your base color, once blue is added, the color is never the same again. In other words, anyone that has ever met me was forever changed. I have the power to be the change, no matter the situation or the circumstances.

If I were a flower, I would be a rose, because a rose comes in many colors, and it can be given for many reasons. I tend to become whatever is needed, whether it's for friendship, encouragement, listening, motivation or the wind beneath someone's wing. I serve my purpose wholeheartedly, but no matter what, a rose is always given in love. I also, like a rose, that seems so beautiful to the eye, can have thorns if not handled carefully. As a rose needs its roots, my roots (family) are fundamental to my existence.

Journey 2/Day 1
Getting to Know Self beyond the Surface

Deeper self-analysis:
An analogy is a similarity in some respects between things that are otherwise dissimilar. How well do you know self? Can you take it to a deeper level? Fill in the blank with the topics below; put some serious thought into it. Your choice answer should represent you, your character and personality.

Note: Please do not think this is about your favorite color or what you look good in, this should reflect you, your character and integrity on a deeper level. Use the template below during your analysis.

If I were a(n)_____, I would be a(n) _____. And tell why?

Animal:
_____
_____
_____

Fruit:
_____
_____
_____

Color:
_____
_____
_____

Flower:
_____
_____
_____

Tool or Instrument: _____
_____
_____

Journey 2/Day 1
Getting to Know Self beyond the Surface

Bonuses: (These were some of my favorite responses when I was doing surveys for the topics above).

One person's Color was Brown because it was the New Black. It was often misunderstood. It was in a class all by itself. It had a purpose but would take a backseat for the sake of others. It had the ability to overshadow anything but did not. It was deep; yet soft.

Another: Flower: Hawaiian paradise because it was delicate yet strong. It was often unknown to many yet had its intended purpose. It was simple; yet, it was bold. It also exuded a certain sign of strength but was always given in love.

Another: Instead of a flower one person was a weed because she grew despite her location. She could take over any or most situations. She had the ability to change any environment. She could choke the life out of anything if need be. She refused to die easily. Sometimes she was even pretty to the eye but bad to those around. She was not necessarily welcomed but that wasn't important. What mattered is that she was present, accounted for and always heard or seen.

You can choose tools or objects. This journey is about you. Remember to stay on the right path.

Other examples: If I were an instrument, I would be a thermostat not a thermometer, because I set the temperature, I don't just measure it.

Another: If I were a tool, I would be a hammer because I am essential to building things even though sometimes I have to tear things down in order to correct mistakes.

And lastly: if I were an automobile, I would be a Range Rover or Rolls Royce. You see, I wouldn't have to advertise and only certain people would have access to me. My presence would be admired from near and far, In other words, one would recognize my status without explanation

In all your doings, be active and open minded;
Think and act outside of the BOX!

Journey 2/Day 1
Getting to Know Self beyond the Surface

Write about a time when you experienced a personal awakening moment. This moment could have been life changing or mind blowing. It forced you to reckon with what was and what was not, in short do some deep thinking and it evoked action on your part. This moment may or may not have caused you to compare self to someone or something else but it caused you to gain perspective of what was to be or what was not to be. This moment either defined or re-defined you. It is said that we are a product of our society, the outcome of what happens to us. Today, I declare and decree that you are no longer the effect but the cause. You are no longer VICTIM but VICTOR!!

_____

_____

_____

_____

_____

_____

_____

_____

_____

_____

_____

_____

_____

_____

_____

_____

_____

_____

Getting to Know Self beyond the Surface

Remembering that moment. Was it tragic or triumphant? Did you take heed or continue to proceed? Call to memory how you felt, how you responded and write about it.

_____

_____

_____

_____

_____

_____

_____

_____

_____

_____

_____

_____

_____

_____

_____

_____

_____

_____

_____

_____

_____

_____

_____

_____

Journey 2/Day 3
Getting to Know Self beyond the Surface

Find your favorite scripture and/or a quote, which gives you strength or encouragement that is empowering. Write it here, then tell why this is your favorite. Describe how it empowers you. You may have more than one, feel free to reflect on a few if you would like. Once you have completed this task, take five minutes to reflect on the key words. Practice at least one of your scriptures or quotes as a daily affirmation.

_____

_____

_____

_____

_____

_____

_____

_____

_____

_____

_____

_____

_____

_____

_____

_____

_____

_____

_____

_____

_____

Journey 2/Day 4
Getting to Know Self beyond the Surface

Visualize then draw or paste magazine images that make you think about strength and overcoming.

Journey 2/Day 5
Getting to Know Self beyond the Surface

Go out and do one of your favorite things that bring you joy and write about it.

_____

_____

_____

_____

_____

_____

_____

_____

_____

_____

_____

_____

_____

_____

_____

_____

_____

_____

_____

_____

_____

_____

_____

Journey 2/Day 6
Getting to Know Self beyond the Surface

Go out and do something that frightens you; fear not for you are not given the spirit of fear but of power and a sound mind. Don't forget to write about it.

_____

_____

_____

_____

_____

_____

_____

_____

_____

_____

_____

_____

_____

_____

_____

_____

_____

_____

_____

_____

_____

_____

Journey 2/Day 7
Getting to Know Self beyond the Surface

Reflection: How did it go this week? What worked, what didn't, and how did it all feel?

_____

_____

_____

_____

_____

_____

_____

_____

_____

_____

_____

_____

_____

_____

_____

_____

_____

_____

_____

_____

_____

_____

_____

The "Who" in Who I Am; your wakeup call

Journey 3/Day 1

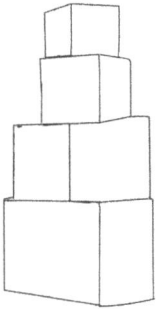

In this next journey you will reflect and begin to reestablish self. This next journey will cause you to wake up and smell the roses. You will see things as they are and not through rose colored glasses. In case you haven't had any rose-colored glasses, they make everything appear as if everything is alright. Please know that if things are not so rosey, that's ok. Ask why not and decide what you are going to do about it. This could be an ending place or starting place, whatever is needed or desired. Make the most of it now! This week I want you to reflect on one of my personal quotes: "without trials or tribulations there will be no triumphs." In other words, without a story, you would have no glory.

My story in short: I was motherless at 7 and fatherless by 12. I was a victim of rape, incest, and molestation. I survived falling out of a speeding car and was skinned almost to the bone. I have been promiscuous, I have been lied on, lied to, cheated on, made to feel worthless or less than while all the time I was being prepared to be taught that I am a child of God, created in his image, one of his wondrous works and created with a purpose.

There have also been times in my life when I knew I was headed in the wrong direction or knew he was Mr. Wrong from the first moment, but I didn't change gears. It was only a matter of time or wasted years that I would never get back. In other words, I didn't value my own time. I had a friend once tell me that we have "uh oh moments" and "ah ha moments"; you might call them emergency exits. Either way, you will eventually learn to take heed and not proceed.

Truth be told, although I was of age, on the inside, I was still a broken, hurt, misguided and lost little girl. I sought love in the wrong places. I justified and validated misuse and abuse for so many years, seeming courageous to only battle with my own fears and insecurities. I escaped the dark road of depression and headed to the light just in the nick of time. I could go on and on about the sad things that happened in my life but I choose not to. Instead, I choose to tell you that I made it! Know and trust that which does not kill you will make you stronger! To God be the Glory!!!!!!

In a brief statement, write what you think of your life so far. Have you lived or have you merely existed? Be honest, this is a way for you to gain perspective, adjust, or adapt.

_____

_____

_____

What accomplishments have you made, of which are you most proud?

_____

_____

_____

How do you think the world sees you? Do you care?

_____

_____

_____

If you allowed yourself to dream, write out how your life would be: Dream BIG!

_____

_____

_____

Journey 3/Day 1
The Who in Who You Are; Your Wakeup Call

How do you feel about yourself?

_____

_____

_____

Write a word that describes you. Be honest.

_____

_____

_____

Where are you now? Clubbing, playing church, both, experimenting, doing you, etc.?

_____

_____

_____

Where do you want to be in the next year? (Do you have an action plan?)

_____

_____

_____

Next 5 years:

_____

_____

_____

Next 10 years:

_____

_____

_____

If you are single, is it by choice or reduced options? (In effort not to offend, what I mean is, do you go where the other singles or like-minded people go, do you do what like-minded people do? You can't be seen if you don't come out of hiding.

_____

_____

_____

The Who in Who You Are; Your Wakeup Call

If in a relationship, how do you describe it? Note: No relationship is bad; if it doesn't give you what you want it will show you what you don't want).

_____

_____

_____

What do you want from the relationship? Do you even know?

_____

_____

_____

What do you bring to it? Are you required to bring anything to the table?

_____

_____

_____

What do you take away from it?

_____

_____

_____

Does it help to balance you, or tear you down?

_____

_____

_____

What do you require? (On any level)

_____

_____

_____

Journey 3/Day 2
The "Who" in Who You Are; Your Wakeup Call

Write about a time when you had a revelation or shall I say an "Ah Ha or Uh oh" moment. That moment you should have escaped or that moment you should have grabbed the bull by the horns and held on for dear life. This could have also been the moment you realized you were not all you thought you were.

_____

_____

_____

_____

_____

_____

_____

_____

_____

_____

_____

_____

_____

_____

_____

_____

_____

_____

_____

_____

Journey 3/Day 2
The Who in Who You Are; Your Wakeup Call

Did you respond or did you react to your "ah ha or Uh oh" moment? Did you simply act as though your wake up moment never happened?

_____

_____

_____

_____

_____

_____

_____

_____

_____

_____

_____

_____

_____

_____

_____

_____

_____

_____

_____

_____

_____

_____

_____

_____

The Who in Who You Are; Your Wakeup Call

Read a scripture or find a quote that will cause you to "wake up and smell the roses." You can also choose to find a scripture or quote that speaks to your current situation. All that I ask is that you do it in a timely manner. Time waits for no one. Time is a valuable yet often misused and abused gift. We tend to take it for granted, thinking that there is always tomorrow. I like to think of the clay in the Potter's hand, sometimes you have to be remolded and reshaped, but keep in mind as you are being remolded or reshaped, time is not.

_____

_____

_____

_____

_____

_____

_____

_____

_____

_____

_____

_____

_____

_____

_____

_____

_____

_____

_____

_____

Journey 3/Day 4
The Who in Who You Are; Your Wakeup Call

Visualize then draw or paste magazine images here that remind you of change or new beginnings. For some, it might even be an ending.

The Who in Who You Are; Your Wakeup Call

Do something that you love, one of your favorite simple pleasures. It might be enjoying the gift of time. Sit and gaze into a river, view a sunrise, sunset, sit in a park and watch children play or simply admire the gift of nature in its natural form. Write about it, tell what you observed. Did you allow yourself to truly embrace the moment? How did you feel? Did it yield your thoughts to a higher power? Did it make you appreciate the simple things in life? Did your attitude become one of gratitude?

_____

_____

_____

_____

_____

_____

_____

_____

_____

_____

_____

_____

_____

_____

_____

_____

_____

_____

_____

Journey 3/Day 6
The "Who" in Who You Are; Your Wakeup Call

Go out and do something that frightens you; conquer a small mountain (If you are like me, you might not have to leave the house, lol.)

_____

_____

_____

_____

_____

_____

_____

_____

_____

_____

_____

_____

_____

_____

_____

_____

_____

_____

_____

_____

_____

_____

_____

The "Who" in Who You Are; Your Wakeup Call

Reflection: How did it go this week? What worked, what didn't, and how did it all feel?

_____

_____

_____

_____

_____

_____

_____

_____

_____

_____

_____

_____

_____

_____

_____

_____

_____

_____

_____

_____

_____

_____

_____

_____

ACCEPTANCE.

Acceptance is accepting what is and what is not. It is not sugarcoating or fluffing. It means you will now deal with reality, consciously. Acceptance is an extension of patience. Patience adds ease and peace in your life. Your frustrations will decrease as your patience increases. Lack of acceptance puts you at great risk for disappointment and conflict. Acceptance will create a more patient and peaceful you, which in turn opens your heart, mind, body, and soul to new state of being. Your struggles will result in strength and your messes will become your message.

Journey 4/Day 1

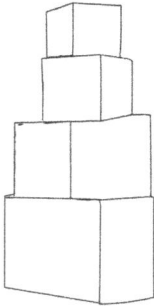

I was still single with a career but feeling unlovable. The worth that had always been determined by others was now up to me, so I had to do some assessing. I was in my twenties, no children, a career, decent income yet questionable credit. I was in a rental house with shag carpet that I hated and my car was in someone else's name building someone's credit. I had set out to do what I wanted to do but shall I say I veered off course. I could afford expensive things, so I tried to cover up the hurt and pain with the best of the best, always DIVAFIED!

Shall I say that I was a dressed up mess! I once told someone else this while we were in a heated argument. I guess the words boomeranged back to me, because I heard myself. Truth be told and truth being accepted, I was a dressed up mess too! Fragmented pieces held together by glue and it was the cheap glue. I managed to function day-to-day. Most people thought I had it all together. I was a busy bee, functionally dysfunction. That was OK; after all, I was not on drugs, alcohol, nor a criminal. No, I was a law abiding registered voter. I never really looked in the mirror and allowed myself to see the parentless child, the hurt young lady, and the lost soul. Don't get me wrong, I was a card carrying DIVA!!!!!!!!!!!

I had even managed to fool myself. One day while traveling back from my hometown, I thought I was having a heart attack. Shall we say anxiety? I had one of my best friends on the phone updating her at various mile markers, just in case. I made it home and made an appointment to see my doctor. As I was
waiting in the doctor's office, I worked on various items from the office. It wasn't even my work, I was making sure things ran smoothly for my boss.

As I waited in the room, the nurse came in and we realized we had worked together previously at a different location. I didn't think she really liked me then but today she was oh so attentive. She began to tell me things about me and for some reason I was in agreement. She seemed to know me oh so well. She said, "Are you stressed at work? Are you overwhelmed? Are you worried about family? Do you cry all the time? Do you even cry when the Taco Bell commercial comes on?" I was like, yes, yes, yes and YES! She said, "Girl you are depressed. You need to ask the doctor for an antidepressant. I know this cause I take them, I have been depressed for years."

I thought she must be right. So I made my case when the doctor came in and she wrote that prescription without hesitation. I had always heard it was hard to get doctors to give out certain types of medication, especially antidepressants, not so! This was easy. Why hadn't I known about this before? So I was off, going to fix myself and my problems with this little pill. She even gave me time off from work, you know an early pre-approved and no questions asked vacation. I left there on cloud nine because everything was going to be alright.

Journey 4/Day 1
ACCEPTANCE.

Zoloft was the answer. It is such an effective drug; you transition to your recommended dose. You have to ease it in your system…1, 2, 5 then 10 milligrams; it takes a couple of weeks. It will prevent anxiety and give you energy. Ok, here we go, I took the first, second and third dose and I was ready to climb in the bed and pull the covers over my head. I didn't care if I ate, bathed, or even returned to work. My family brought food, money and whatever they thought I needed or wanted. Then they sat and talked and talked and talked. I was like "blah, blah, blah, leave, leave, leave." Then it happened, the last one was leaving, I turned the lights out as I ushered him to the door. To the bed I went. So I get up Thursday night and I am like what is going on. I started thinking about my future "Past" medical history and it read depression, etc. I looked in the mirror and reflected on a play I had seen by Millie Jackson and said I am taking my life back. I called the doctor the next morning and ask what the medicine should be doing. She said it should ease your mind and give you lots and lots of energy. I explained what it had done to me and I hadn't had a true dose yet, and she said come back in and we will try something else. I said no, we will not and I will be ok. It has been twenty plus years and I keep that same package of Zoloft in the drawer of my nightstand as a reminder that I am okay and I can take control at any time. Besides, if someone willingly draws a conclusion for you, you need to step back and really look at the situation. Nobody knows you better than you.

I began to reflect over my life and I thought about a time I visited a church in Philadelphia. It was a different type of church and it had a different feeling than what I was accustomed to. The Minister and his team would come to you and ask if you mind them praying for you and if you didn't mind, you would go up to the front and the team would prophesy to you. What was neat is they recorded it and gave you the recording to keep. During my time, one of the ladies told me how I had been hurt, one spoke of surety, one spoke of my heart and how God knew my heart, my secrets, my pains because HE made me. The other told me that I would find myself crying even when I didn't have a reason. She told me that God wanted me to know that He was not through with me and at these times He was working on me. I just need to trust and know that God was working on me. I searched and found my tape and began to play it over and over from time to time. I began to listen to it and apply it to my life. I never needed any medication and my life began to change.

First, I had to come to grips with who I was and who I wasn't on the inside and out. I had to accept that I had been lied to and on. I had to accept I had been cheated on and my heart was now bruised and hardened. I had to accept that my childhood woes would not extend adulthood woes. I even had to accept that I didn't have it all together and needed help in the worst way. I also had to accept I wasn't in control, God was. I had to accept that just because I wasn't what I had been, I wasn't what I needed to be. I had to accept that I couldn't save everybody because I needed saving. I had to understand that when someone said they liked me it was NOT love. I had to know and accept that love is and should not be conditional, given or received. I accepted that I wasn't the prettiest or the finest woman but whatever I was God created me that way. I didn't have an addiction but I did need recovery. I realized acceptance leads to acknowledgement. Acknowledgment renders that there is a problem and you need help. Seeking help puts you in the way of amends. Amends sets you on the path to recovery. Recovery is ongoing and infinite. You can tell someone who is recovered. They are on their second walk. They are appreciative. They have sincere gratitude. They don't take people or things for granted. They notice and appreciate the smaller things in life. Life becomes beautiful and you begin to live a blessed and more abundant life. You find yourself paying attention to the finer details in life. You care about what never really mattered before. You start to have a voice and you stop being afraid to use it. In fact, you start liking to hear yourself talk. You really appreciate being heard. You realize that your presence makes a difference. You begin to re-define yourself while learning to accept and embrace all that has happened to you. You cease to be a victim and start becoming a victor. You might not need 12 steps but you must be willing to go take the first step of Acceptance! This is crucial and important in your transition I will give you a few things that I call my basic toolkit. There may be other ways or things that you use but please remember to pick up your toolkit and get MOVED. Remember the race is not given to the swift but to the one who perseveres. I believe you will do just fine.

~Twelve steps to getting M.O.V.E.D. ~

- Make up your mind that there is a problem
- Decide to make a change
- Create an action plan for change
- Set a goal, make it personal
- Go after it with vengeance
- Remain steadfast and focused
- Make your vision bigger than your fear
- Setup a strong and solid foundation
- Move on purpose with a purpose
- Understand your desired outcome
- Count it all Joy, Live hard and love harder!!
- Share it and allow your story to manifest your glory!!!!!

ACCEPTANCE

The Toolkit
(Remember to use the your twelve steps and toolkit daily during this journey)

My purpose is to awaken, encourage, inspire, aspire, motivate and move with you. My purpose is to show that you have a purpose and that you are not here by accident; you did not get here by coincidence, but instead by experience. Experience is life's greatest teacher; age is how we pay for it. Pain and strife are taxes pre-collected. But life with a purpose is our benefit. I will give you some advice, but more importantly I will give you the tools to make it happen. I first want you to learn the serenity prayer, because the word accept is so huge, it is your bridge. The second tool is faith because you will have to rely on the unseen, and without work, this will all be in vain. Last, I want you to seek joy, a spirit gift from God. Put down the happy and unhappy because they are temporary. Joy is everlasting.

Tool #1: Serenity Prayer
"God grant me the serenity to accept the things I cannot change; courage to change the things I can; and wisdom to know the difference. Living one day at a time; Enjoying one moment at a time; Accepting hardships as the pathway to peace; Taking, as He did, this sinful world as it is, not as I would have it; Trusting that He will make all things right. If I surrender to His will; So that I may be the reasonably happy in his life, and supremely happy with Him Forever and ever in the next. - Amen"

Tool #2: Scripture on Faith
Faith is the substance of things hoped for, the evidence of things not seen. -
Hebrews 11:1

Tool #3: Meditate on Joy
Joy is simple yet hard for some to find. Joy is unspeakable. Joy is that thing that gives you peace in the mist of your storm.

Tool #4: Self-Acceptance
It is an absolute must that you learn to accept who you are as well as who you are not! Acceptance is a small word that is megalithic. It can make or break you or your situation.

Journey 4/Day 1
ACCEPTANCE

They say a picture is worth a thousand words. Or they say, "Take a picture, it will last longer." You can also draw a picture here. Do whatever is easiest. The picture should represent how you truly see yourself un-retouched. Make sure it encompasses the good, bad and ugly. Most importantly be honest. If you are fat, leave off the spanx, let the rolls show. If you are queenly, draw a crown but if you are nosey make sure you show your beak. Maybe you have a crocodile's snout because your mouth is so treacherous. Maybe you have a halo because you give unselfishly. Your heart might be broken, mended or huge, make sure you capture the real you.

Place or draw your picture here: Make sure it is not a glamour or re-touched photo.

(This can be a candid shot, unprofessional quick print or a simple drawing. Make sure your perception is illustrated in reality. In other words, big hand-giver, heart-lover, smile-cheerful.) BE HONEST!

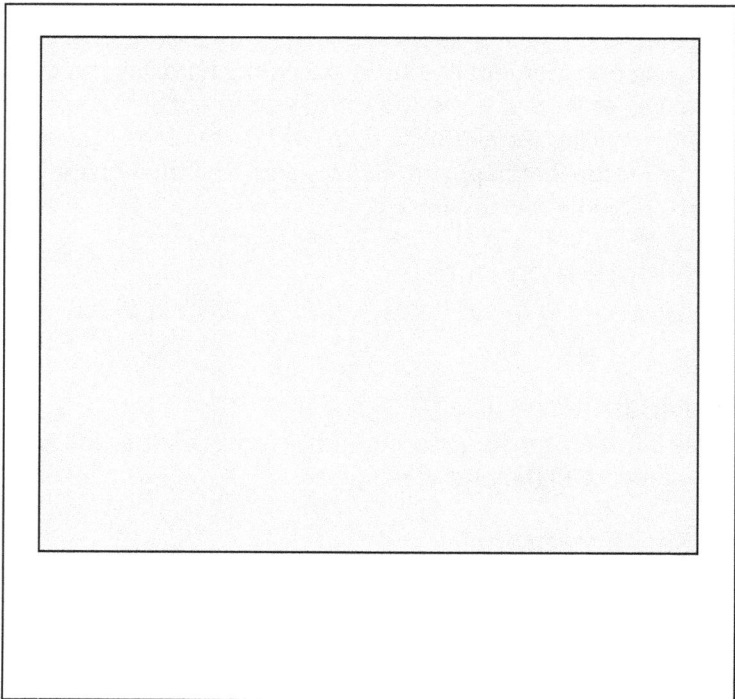

Journey 4/Day 1
ACCEPTANCE

Write about a time when you had to face the facts about a certain situation. You may have been at wits end or wanted to give up but you didn't.

_____

_____

_____

_____

_____

_____

_____

_____

_____

_____

_____

_____

_____

_____

_____

_____

_____

_____

_____

_____

_____

_____

_____

_____

Journey 4/Day 2
ACCEPTANCE

Write about a time you had to accept the hand you were dealt. Are you truly over it or are you still dealing with it. If you escaped, great! If not, why not? How did or will you deal with it? You must hurt before you can heal. You must make a conscience decision and the time is now!

_____

_____

_____

_____

_____

_____

_____

_____

_____

_____

_____

_____

_____

_____

_____

_____

_____

_____

_____

_____

Journey 4/Day 3
ACCEPTANCE

Write your favorite scripture or quote that is about acceptance. Next, look back and review the "Modified Twelve Step Program." Please note, it has been modified because you may not have used drugs, alcohol, or any other substance; however, we are all recovering from something. After you have re-read the 12 steps, take time to jot down where you think you are. After assessing your current situation, write down a plan and begin to map out your victory.

_____

_____

_____

_____

_____

_____

_____

_____

_____

_____

_____

_____

_____

_____

_____

_____

_____

_____

_____

_____

Journey 4/Day 4
ACCEPTANCE

Visualize then draw or paste magazine images here that represent various type(s) of situation/struggles you have or are currently dealing with.

Journey 4/Day 5
ACCEPTANCE

You survived it, you must now tell it,! You will learn that acceptance will lend towards sharing. As you share your story, you will help others while helping self. You will loose strongholds and bondage that held you captive for years. You will feel better and so relieved. You will be able to motivate others and become empowered on a new level. Know that which does not kill you will make you stronger! Remember to write your experience.

_____

_____

_____

_____

_____

_____

_____

_____

_____

_____

_____

_____

_____

_____

_____

_____

_____

Journey 4/Day 6
ACCEPTANCE

Challenge: Go out and do something to encourage or help someone. This could be a need or a kind gesture; the goal is to make a difference. Observe their reaction. How did it affect you? How did you feel? Know that this action does not have to be financial; it can be encouraging words, hugs, smiles or even a compassionate touch. Make today about unsolicited help. Write about the experience.

_____

_____

_____

_____

_____

_____

_____

_____

_____

_____

_____

_____

_____

_____

_____

_____

_____

_____

_____

Reflection: how did it go this week? What worked, what didn't, and how did it all feel?

_____

_____

_____

_____

_____

_____

_____

_____

_____

_____

_____

_____

_____

_____

_____

_____

_____

_____

_____

_____

_____

Congratulations, you've completed one month. Only two months to go until you reach the next season...

Learning to Respect and Love Self

Journey 5/Day 1

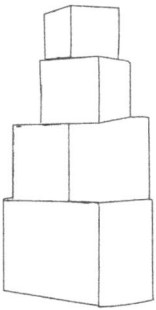

For many years, I felt as if I had to do for people when and wherever. I thought it was my job. I gave and gave and gave at the cost of sacrificing myself. I had to get validation through other people and their opinions mattered. I fell prey to friends, family, peers and men. It is so easy to do what everyone else does, but it is hard to stand alone. You find yourself wandering aimlessly and you become a target. I never really thought I was the problem, if there was a problem; it had to be someone else.

Even after surviving rape, incest and molestation, I didn't realize that I was a survivor. I truly existed.

People could tell me anything. Men could make me believe anything and I really believed they were all good or shall I say at least good for one thing, LOL! So in short, two things caused my next setback: lack of self-respect and lack of love for self! Again, I could go on and on but in effort to keep you on time and task I will shorten my crisis. I was now getting it right and thought I had it together; I had finally saved some money, got out of that rental house with that shag carpet. Yes, I bought my first home! I was even working on buying a car in my name. I had practiced abstinence for several years just because. My family had always gotten together for dinner around the holidays. However, this year was different. I had just bought my first home and dinner would be at my house. I loved to stay up all night and cook; it's just what I do. The doorbell rings and this time a guy I had known, that had chased me over the years, shows up with my brother in law. His conversation was different and he seemed more mature than I remembered. We started dating and things went great!

Well, there soon came my price to pay. My life was about to change forever. I dated him, became pregnant and a statistic. I was now pregnant out of wedlock, a single parent to be with a future absent father. No matter how hard I tried to explain it to myself, this was a situation I didn't expect nor did I think I could initially survive. My mind told me I was a statistic. I was no better than anyone else. I thought he loved me, I thought he cared? God how? God why? Protect me oh Lord, make a way out of no way, please! This was too much to bear. How, why, not me? I later realized that it was a blessing and my turning point. My struggle fueled my strength. My strength fueled my faith and my Faith fueled my walk with God. It was my storyline that lead me to my glory line.

I was no longer my situation. I realized Gold goes through the fire and a Diamond starts in the ruff. Your words change your thoughts and your thoughts change your heart.

You could probably put people in categories if asked but instead ask yourself, what really matters most? Does the good outweigh the bad? Or does the bad outweigh the good? Or is there balance? To know or not know will make all the difference in the upcoming weeks. The key here is to know that no matter where you fall in life, you still have both good and bad qualities. No one is perfect and without faults or flaws. What is important is having self-value, self-worth, self-love and self-respect. If you possess these qualities, they will automatically overflow to others in and/or around you.

You have done a great job. You have made some progress and I am proud you did not put this book down for two reasons: 1.) you want more for yourself and 2.) you now know you deserve more. In your next assignment I ask you to think on the terms self, selfish, selflessness and self-full. Then I ask you to think about respect. Do you know people who are selfish, selfless, self-full, respectful, and/or disrespectful? Take a few minutes to put some of them in the categories on the next page.

Here is an example of defining self, selfish, selfless, self-full:

Self: Simply you. No make-believes. No extras.

Selfish: If it doesn't benefit you, you're not interested.

Selfless: You are here to please, serve and satisfy all others; forsaking self.

Self-full: One who values self-first and foremost!

Note: This is for your eyes only so be honest, if you are sharing use code names.

Self	Selfish	Selfless	Self-full

The goal should be "Self-full". You can't give what you don't have. You can't give from an empty place!"

Journey 5/Day 1
Learning to Respect and Love Self

When I think about respect, I think of something my Dad did when I was a child. His one action taught me about respect. I was in our neighborhood liquor store and Lacey, the neighborhood drunk, came in. He was already good and tipsy. The owner was there and he was talking to some other white men in suits, they seemed all too important, he barely noticed me. Lacey kept asking for a bottle and the owner kept ignoring him. After a few more attempts, the owner cursed Lacey bad. I ran out the store and told my Dad about it. My dad took all of us to the front of the store and he rallied for all the people around to come over. He then drew an imaginary line with his foot and told us not to cross it for any reason. This meant everyone, young and old. He said we better not buy a piece of 1-cent candy until the owner apologized publicly to Lacey. He said it didn't matter if he was a drunk, Lacey was still a man and that's all that mattered. After a couple of days or a week or so, the owner came out front and publicly apologized to Lacey in front of all the people. Lacey had a smile as big as Mississippi. Now that's demanding respect.

Do you respect yourself?

_____

_____

_____

Do you respect others?

_____

_____

_____

If disrespected, what do you do?

_____

_____

_____

Journey 5/Day 1
Learning to Respect and Love Self

Write about a time when you did something for someone else or stood up for yourself.

_____

_____

_____

_____

_____

_____

_____

_____

_____

_____

_____

_____

_____

_____

_____

_____

_____

_____

_____

_____

_____

_____

_____

Journey 5/Day 2
Learning to Respect and Love Self

Write about any strongholds or longsuffering that you have dealt with. Did you reach a breaking point? Do you feel bound? Know that anything that binds you, controls you.

_____

_____

_____

_____

_____

_____

_____

_____

_____

_____

_____

_____

_____

_____

_____

_____

_____

_____

_____

_____

_____

_____

_____

Journey 5/Day 3
Learning to Respect and Love Self

How did you feel? Did your action birth a new you, change you or activate a new level of respect?

_____

_____

_____

_____

_____

_____

_____

_____

_____

_____

_____

_____

_____

_____

_____

_____

_____

_____

_____

_____

_____

_____

Journey 5/Day 4
Learning to Respect and Love Self

Write about a time when you failed yourself or someone else? Why didn't you do something?

_____

_____

_____

_____

_____

_____

_____

_____

_____

_____

_____

_____

_____

_____

_____

_____

_____

_____

_____

_____

_____

_____

Journey 5/Day 5
Learning to Respect and Love Self

Have you forgiven yourself? If not, please do so now. Write down some of the shoulda, coulda, wouldas. Now say this, then write it: I forgive myself for what I didn't do, I forgive myself for what I did do because I am learning to love and respect myself regardless of. This is a turning point, TURN NOW!!!!

_____

_____

_____

_____

_____

_____

_____

_____

_____

_____

_____

_____

_____

_____

_____

_____

_____

_____

_____

_____

_____

Journey 5/Day 6
Learning to Respect and Love Self

It is important to give back but it really is rewarding when it is close to your heart. Look back over your life, what area did someone pour into your Spirit? Using that as a foundation, find a cause or group that is dear to your heart that will benefits others; a church, public or community service group, VOLUNTEER! Write about your reflection, your action and the affect it had on you.

_____

_____

_____

_____

_____

_____

_____

_____

_____

_____

_____

_____

_____

_____

_____

_____

_____

_____

_____

_____

Journey 5/Day 7
Learning to Respect and Love Self

Do something just for yourself, then reflect on this past week, how did it go, what did or didn't you like?

_____

_____

_____

_____

_____

_____

_____

_____

_____

_____

_____

_____

_____

_____

_____

_____

_____

_____

_____

_____

_____

_____

_____

_____

Journey 6/Day 1
Learning to Move With a Purpose

Yippee!!!!!!!!!!!!!! We have made progress.Now we must move however, whenever and wherever. We need to move. Movement means we are making progress, correct? Wrong.......................... it means you are moving. However, you must have a purpose for which you move!!!!!

Journey 6/Day 1

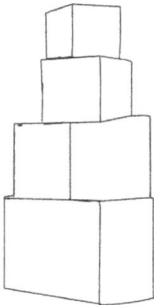

I began to move with a vengeance, no one was going to stop me. I just needed to get things done; I think I called them goals. I validated my reason for whatever I chose to do without thought or merit. I began to do things but with an elevated authority and reason. I started and finished Beauty School, worked in a salon, this DIVA was reigning again. I was a weave master in the beauty shop and my career was great too! I felt that I had balance because on my day job, the people had problems but they were sick. It was fine because in the evenings and on weekends, my clients had problems but they were well. Well, not really. No matter what people thought, I thought I was good and that's what mattered. I seem to start to have a vision and could even deal with some let downs that didn't break me down. My family was great, my friends were great and my social life wasn't bad either. I could wear the top name clothing and accessories and my hair and nails were always on point. I opened and closed one of the local clubs most weekends. I was single and boy did I mingle. I even told myself that a married man was best. I somehow convinced myself he would be best because I didn't have to buy him anything because he couldn't take it home. Don't get me wrong, I was never messy and the Mrs. Was off limits. To say the least, I guess I had misconstrued morals. Secondly, I would not have to deal with him all of the time and the holidays were mine to do with them as I pleased.

I never really liked drinking but I would dance the night away. I knew I was a temptation and it did my ego well to temp as many as I could. I was your everyday girlie girl elevated to the 10th power; I could shoot pool, and I could talk sports, politics, current events, etc. You name it, I claimed it. I was not going to be left out and I made sure I was heard. Family and friends first, all else was a bonus.

I started having myself a proclaimed day, week and month. I made a pact with myself to travel two to three states a year. I rallied in the fact that when I had drank, ate or slept, my family had drank, ate or slept. It was all about me!

I still did what needed to be done for others and helped whenever I needed to, but it was still really about me, or so I wanted to believe. It made me feel better not whole. It seemed to be a placebo that worked temporarily for me until the next situation came along. You see, I numbed the pain and created a scab over all my wounds because I had to do what I had to do in order to keep it moving. You know the ole phrase, "keep it moving" and "make it do what it do." For once, I finally had some control and was in the driver's seat. Or shall I say, so I thought. I must admit life seemed to be going well I was getting all the bumps and bruises I had before, but I minimized the effect others had on me. I was going to be a key deciding factor in how things would go from now on, boy was I wrong!

I had dreams but no real vision or goals. My moving only stirred the dust, it didn't make new track

Journey 6/Day 1
Learning to Move With a Purpose

What is your purpose for moving?

_____

_____

Personal Goals can be: A happy marriage, a great family, a great body, single yet satisfied, etc.

_____

_____

Professional Goals can be: success, money, career, clout, reputation, entrepreneurship, etc.

_____

_____

What are some of your Struggles: procrastination, denial, judgment, low self-esteem, immaturity, negligence, dishonesty with self, trapped, stagnation, etc.

_____

_____

Note: you are allowed to dream, just remember that a goal has a date. It is imperative that you know the difference and that you always aim high. Get busy living and stop existing.

_____

_____

GET M.O.V.E.D.

What are your goals?

_____

_____

_____

_____

Personal Goal:

_____

_____

_____

_____

_____

_____

_____

_____

Professional Goals:

_____

_____

_____

_____

_____

_____

_____

_____

Journey 6/Day 1

Learning to Move With a Purpose

Write about a time when you set and achieved a goal (Big or Small); how did you feel?

_____

_____

_____

_____

_____

_____

_____

_____

_____

_____

_____

_____

_____

_____

_____

_____

_____

_____

_____

_____

_____

_____

Journey 6/Day 2
Learning to Move With a Purpose

Write about a time when you thought you were in control, but realized later that you weren't, how did you feel? How did you handle the situation?

_____

_____

_____

_____

_____

_____

_____

_____

_____

_____

_____

_____

_____

_____

_____

_____

_____

_____

_____

_____

_____

_____

_____

_____

_____

Journey 6/Day 3
Learning to Move With a Purpose

Reference a scripture or quote that speaks to who is really in control of your destiny. Write about your beliefs. Tell whether or not this is your true belief or your inherited belief. As you mature, you develop a sense of principles that become your foundation of existence. Have your beliefs remained the same or have they altered?

_____

_____

_____

_____

_____

_____

_____

_____

_____

_____

_____

_____

_____

_____

_____

_____

_____

_____

_____

_____

Journey 6/Day 4
Learning to Move With a Purpose

Write a short letter to yourself and talk about what you thought your purposes or destiny was as a young child. Then write another letter and talk about what you now believe your destiny is an adult. How have they changed or did your views remain the same. Don't forget to record your results.

_____

_____

_____

_____

_____

_____

_____

_____

_____

_____

_____

_____

_____

_____

_____

_____

_____

_____

_____

_____

_____

_____

_____

_____

Journey 6/Day 5
Learning to Move With a Purpose

Go out and do one of your favorite things that involve your true passion. Now write about it.

_____

_____

_____

_____

_____

_____

_____

_____

_____

_____

_____

_____

_____

_____

_____

_____

_____

_____

_____

_____

_____

_____

_____

Journey 6/Day 6
Learning to Move With a Purpose

Challenge: Go out and do something that frightens you so that you learn to move boldly. Now write about it.

_____

_____

_____

_____

_____

_____

_____

_____

_____

_____

_____

_____

_____

_____

_____

_____

_____

_____

_____

_____

_____

_____

_____

Journey 6/Day 7
Learning to Move With a Purpose

Reflection: How did it go this week? What worked, what didn't, and how did it all feel? Write about it.

_____

_____

_____

_____

_____

_____

_____

_____

_____

_____

_____

_____

_____

_____

_____

_____

_____

_____

_____

_____

_____

_____

Positive Perspective

"No matter how low you get, there is always someone that is just a little bit lower than you." These are wise words from my Aunt Tommie that kept me from giving in or up. I had some very low points but those few words never allowed me to see myself at the lowest. This was my saving grace. I had an Aunt Annie Mae that always said I love you and I pray for you every day. This allowed me to know I had someone who cared even though they were not in sight. Don't get me wrong, I had many people, young and old, that would lend support but it really was up to me. How did I look at things? What was my perception? Who or what made the difference?

Journey 7/Day 1

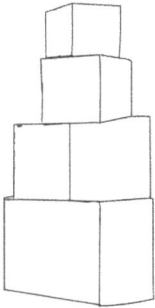

Our perspective equals our outlook and in most cases our outcome. No one or anything else really matters. Our perspective is the key to our getting MOVED! It can and will affect us either positively or negatively.

In short, know who you are. As I mentioned before, my Mom died when I was 7 and my Dad was killed when I was 12. I did some things I am not proud of but there are a lot of things I have done that I am very proud of. The reason why good outweighed and outlasted the bad was mainly because I knew my Father and what he stood for. His legacy lived on through my siblings and myself. He stood for integrity, service, commitment, loyalty, respect and love. I knew what I was made of, I just had to accept it and walk in it.

We must see the bigger picture; it's not just about us. Know not only who you are but whose you are. Know your purpose and start to walk in it. Start with the person in the mirror.

This week you will simply concentrate on the right perspective. Your goal will be to have a positive perspective. The bible says that so shall the mind thinketh the heart will grow it. Know that there is power in the tongue, so be careful what you speak!

Name one thing that you love about your life that keeps you going. This is about you and you alone...not your family, children, spouse or job. YOU!!!! It's simple; this is about you and you alone. Besides, if you can't find one thing about yourself, we really have work to do!

_____

_____

_____

_____

_____

_____

_____

_____

What is important to you: your today or your tomorrow? Why?

_____

_____

_____

_____

_____

_____

_____

_____

Positive Perspective

What does your life, thus far, say about you?

_____

_____

_____

_____

_____

_____

_____

What is a legacy? What will they say when we are no longer around? Did you serve a purpose? Will anyone speak of you or will you be a simple or everlasting memory for generations to come? Will the life you live speak for you? What do you want your legacy to be?

_____

_____

_____

_____

_____

_____

_____

Note: My hope is that my legacy will be the essence of my character and my being. It shall live on and my family and my friends for years to come. Through my child and her children's children, shall my rich legacy dwell. My legacy shall not be trimmed out in tradition but cherished and highly esteemed due to

God, my way of loving, rich love for life, and people. It will signify changes for the better and help for the needy.

Meditate on this for a moment: "I give thanks to you, for I am awesomely and wondrously made! Wondrous are your works, and my being knows it well."

Be real with yourself. Have you ever really thought on this? Do you believe what it says? Can you allow this to be the core of your thoughts? Knowing this from your inner being and core existence will cause you to evolve on a whole new level.

Be honest with yourself. Can you? Have you? If not, pledge now to be honest from this point on!   Know that being honest isn't always pretty and exciting. Sometimes being truly honest is ugly and painful. Consider it a long overdue pruning; one must be pruned to rid itself of the lifeless things in order to sprout new things.

Journey 7/Day 1
Positive Perspective

Retrospective Glance

First, list three of your favorite childhood memories: (This allows you to look back and see our past without holding on to baggage instead referencing your history).

_____

_____

_____

_____

Secondly, go back to where you found happiness; you know that state where all is well, even the simple/silly things. List them here:

_____

_____

_____

_____

Third, I want you to list a few "steal away moments." That is what I called the memories that before things got complicated, life was simple. Life didn't require much of us and we embraced life on a major level. As responsibilities grew, our embrace on life withered. Sometimes it becomes necessary to go back in time, mentally. The thoughts of the good ole days often give us a feeling of joy. So we should practice going back from time to time.

For example:
1. My steal away moment would be going to a neighborhood store and paying a dollar for penny candy--- seemed like a million pieces, I know right?

2. When my mom and her friends would be getting ready to go out and they would put us on the table and we would practice the dance moves: the hustle, the tilt, and the robot. That was a party in my eyes.

3. Hearing my grandfather singing the ole gospel songs as he bopped us on his knee. My favorites were: *Mary Don't You Weep* and *If I Got My Ticket Lord, Can I Ride?*

4. Last but not least, my dad doing his one-leg hop across the room on a good day, you knew the "House" did well! Only a hustler's child would understand this. Lol.

List a few of your "steal away moments"

_____

_____

_____

_____

_____

_____

_____

_____

_____

_____

_____

_____

_____

_____

_____

_____

_____

_____

_____

_____

Journey 7/Day 1
Positive Perspective

Did you enjoy that? It's probably been a while. So many times we get caught up in the 'goings on' of day to day that we become our mate's mate, our children's parent and our job marketing piece. Never meaning to give up the pure essence of who we truly are, we sometimes absorb the personality of others; that sweet loving, caring and important person. In other words, we cease to live and begin to exist. Well guess what, today is your lucky day! Make a banner, highlight it on the calendar, most of all make today your day. Celebrate you; I'll wait while you have a party. *Nothing fancy,* tear up some paper and make it a confetti party! Play some music and party hard!!!!!

Go, Go, Don't' stop, Get it, Get it...Look at ya now!
- Dance like no one is watching
- Sing out loud as if no one is listening
- Choreograph your 1st big number

How did you celebrate? Do tell, what did you do?

_____

_____

_____

_____

_____

_____

_____

_____

_____

_____

_____

_____

_____

_____

Journey 7/Day 1
Positive Perspective

_____

_____

_____

_____

_____

_____

_____

_____

_____

_____

OK, don't hurt yourself.

Thought to ponder on: No matter what piece of the puzzle you are, you are indispensable! You are a part of the whole picture and you make all the difference in the final picture!

Thought to wonder on: Allow your mind, body and soul to be present, not where you are, but where you plan to be. Go see or do something amazing, expose and enlighten yourself.

Thought to linger on: In the darkest moments love yourself enough to be open to someone loving you the way you deserve to be loved!

Journey 7/Day 2
Positive Perspective

Write about a time when you had to start over, change your way of being and/or thinking for the better.

_____

_____

_____

_____

_____

_____

_____

_____

_____

_____

_____

_____

_____

_____

_____

_____

_____

_____

_____

_____

_____

_____

_____

_____

_____

_____

Journey 7/Day 2
Positive Perspective

What did you have to do? What made you do it? What caused your awakening? Was it a move, starting a new job, promotion, leaving a bad relationship, divorce, death, etc. How did you begin to make the best of your new normal?

_____

_____

_____

_____

_____

_____

_____

_____

_____

_____

_____

_____

_____

_____

_____

_____

_____

_____

_____

_____

_____

_____

_____

_____

A Positive Perspective

Write the scripture or quote that got you through your transition. Next, journal why you desire change at this point.

_____

_____

_____

_____

_____

_____

_____

_____

_____

_____

_____

_____

_____

_____

_____

_____

_____

_____

_____

_____

_____

_____

_____

_____

_____

Journey 7/Day 4
A Positive Perspective

Visualize, draw or paste magazine images here that reflect new beginnings or change.

Journey 7/Day 5
Positive Perspective

Go out and do one of your favorite things that celebrate a new change. Write about your experience.

_____

_____

_____

_____

_____

_____

_____

_____

_____

_____

_____

_____

_____

_____

_____

_____

_____

_____

_____

_____

_____

_____

Journey 7/Day 6
Positive Perspective

Go out and do something that will empower you! You are Great! Try on ridiculous expensive clothing, get a makeover, look at fine jewelry, smell expensive perfumes/colognes. Whatever floats your boat to the next level. Don't buy, just take a quick selfie and move on. Now write about it.

_____

_____

_____

_____

_____

_____

_____

_____

_____

_____

_____

_____

_____

_____

_____

_____

_____

_____

_____

_____

_____

_____

Journey 7/Day 7
Positive Perspective

Reflection: How did it go this week? What worked, what didn't, and how did it all feel?

_____

_____

_____

_____

_____

_____

_____

_____

_____

_____

_____

_____

_____

_____

_____

_____

_____

_____

_____

_____

_____

_____

_____

Journey 8/Day 1
Recalibration

Recalibration means reset or an end to something, but it signifies something that you do because it will help you achieve something else. In other words, you get to reset the standards for life.

Here we go... you should be good at this by now. Your theme song says a lot about how you see yourself. What's your choice of music? Will it calm you down or will it build you up?

Journey 8/Day 1

Your statement... what can I say? It's probably too much for words. What do you say about you?

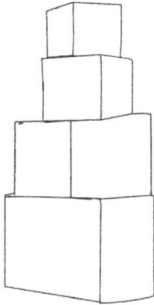

_____

_____

_____

_____

_____

_____

_____

This gets personal; to release some things are to free yourself. It is funny how life works, in one breath your secret keeps you from being revealed to others and their judgment. In another breath, revealing your secret releases you from self-judgment and self-ridicule. This frees you to see that their opinions and judgment never mattered to begin with. WOW!

The reason I asked you to do the exercise in the previous journey was because we must have a clear understanding in order to change our perspective and recalibrate, we must often reflect, re-live and renew.

Scripture states in 1 Corinthians 13:11: When I was a child, I spake as a child, I understood as a child, I thought as a child: but when I became a man, I put away childish things. (KJV)

In other words: growth, maturity and action is mandated. Action negates inaction, therefore you must always be willing to adjust and adapt.

As a child, years after my Mom passed one day my Dad saw an old friend and asked me to go get her, of course I did not, I pretended that I tried. She was not my Mom. Eventually they talked and dated. She was a blessing to all of us. As an young adult before becoming a Mother, I had the mindset that I didn't want anyone with children. As I matured and a gained the right perspective, I realized how wrong my perspective was. My Dad not only wanted and or needed to love he needed to be loved on various levels.

Later when I became pregnant out of wedlock, I felt like I had not only failed myself but I had also failed my family. I had actually become a statistic. To make matters worse, he was looking to be an absent father. Although I knew my daughter would need him, I knew I had to find my inner strength and turn to God. How? Why was this happening to me? I had been a survivor but none of that seemed to matter. My Dad would have never turned his back on his responsibility, how did I not see his true character? Wasn't I smarter than this? I was so judgmental and unforgiving of myself because of my current situation. Don't get me wrong, I loved my child, after all, she was my miracle. I had been told I would never have children. Look at God! In spite of my circumstances I still found a sense of Joy. It wasn't until later (years), I thought back on my life situation and realized that I needed to change my perspective. I was not a single parent; I was a parent who happened to be single. I was not a statistic, instead I set the standard! I also had to realize that even in my dad's absence, after his death, The Father took care of me and HE would take care of my daughter. I had to learn to have a "not yet praise" and lean not to my own understanding but in all ways acknowledge HIM.

Remember EMPOWERMNET is life changing, FORGIVENESS is freeing and MOVEMENT is necessary!!!!!!

A little insight for fun…………….

What is your theme song? _____

Give a one statement from a song that describes you. The real you!_____

_____

If you were a sport, which one would I be and why?_____

_____

If you could change one thing about you, it would be _____ and

why?_____

If you could keep one thing about you it would be: _____

and why? _____

If anyone knew that you: _____
you would be dead or in jail.

If you could take the trip of a lifetime, you would go _____

and why?_____

If you could do something and no one would ever find out, you would _____

_____.

You always wanted to _____

_____.

Let's Dream a little………Let your imagination run WILD!!!!!!!!!!
Your dream job:_____(are you
working in that direction?)

My dream house: _____

_____(give details)

My dream car: _____

_____(give details)

My dream Spouse :_____(don't be afraid to laugh at yourself out loud, I am.)

(Place a picture of your dream car, house, husband, career or whatever.........
Visualize)

Journey 8/Day 1
Recalibration

Write about a time when you surprised yourself, good or bad.

_____

_____

_____

_____

_____

_____

_____

_____

_____

_____

_____

_____

_____

_____

_____

_____

_____

_____

_____

_____

_____

_____

_____

Journey 8/Day 2
Recalibration

How did you feel? Liberated, ashamed, etc ...(let's be honest, not all of us have saved a stray dog)

_____

_____

_____

_____

_____

_____

_____

_____

_____

_____

_____

_____

_____

_____

_____

_____

_____

_____

_____

_____

_____

_____

_____

Journey 8/Day 3
Recalibration

Let's look at caution vs. fear. Caution is indwelled in humankind with the right intention, however as times changed, humankind may not. Caution then becomes fear and you forget to take risks. Are you a risk taker or does caution and fear drive your actions? I believe that I was born a risk taker but somewhere down the line my fears overcame me. Fear limits your ability to achieve. It reduces your tendency to soar.

Draw a line down the middle of this sheet: list your Fears on the Left and list risks you have taken on the right.

_____

_____

_____

_____

_____

_____

_____

_____

_____

_____

_____

_____

Were you surprised by the results?

_____

_____

Journey 8/Day 4
Recalibration

Visualize, draw or paste magazine images here to represent risk takers and freedom.

Journey 8/Day 5
Recalibration

Do something that will give you the feeling of thrill seeking; something out of the ordinary.

_____

_____

_____

_____

_____

_____

_____

_____

_____

_____

_____

_____

_____

_____

_____

_____

_____

_____

_____

_____

_____

_____

Journey 8/Day 6
Recalibration

Go out and do something that frightens/challenges you; it must be something new.

_____

_____

_____

_____

_____

_____

_____

_____

_____

_____

_____

_____

_____

_____

_____

_____

_____

_____

_____

_____

_____

Journey 8/Day 7
Recalibration

Reflection: How did it go this week? What worked, what didn't, and how did it all feel?

_____

_____

_____

_____

_____

_____

_____

_____

_____

_____

_____

_____

_____

_____

_____

_____

_____

_____

_____

_____

_____

_____

MAKING PROGRESS

Congratulations. You've completed two months. Now, you're just one month away from being moved.

Hurting, Healing, Forgiving and Learning to Move Forward

Journey 9/Day 1

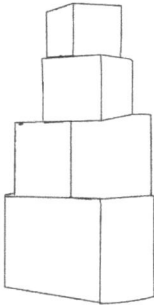

I must say that my life has been a journey that some would not have survived but I did! I wouldn't have wished some of the things that I have experienced on my worst enemy. I thought I was finally where I would be ok. I was doing pretty well and then I found myself confused about what my next step should be. I don't think I took the wrong road but I did think it was for a different reason. Afterwards I found myself in an unfamiliar place. I was now forced to make a decision, a decision that would change the rest of my life. I survived being Motherless, Fatherless, Raped, Molested and a victim of Incest. I had even managed to get through high school, college and Beauty School. I have to admit I cried my way through, but I made it. I was allowing my situation to define me. I was now going to be a single parent and pretty sure the Dad would not be around. How could I let this happen? How did I become another statistic? Not that I was better than anyone else, I just couldn't accept it. Why not?

I was told at the age of twelve that I would not be able to get pregnant or carry a child full term, but I always used some type of precaution. On several occasions, I desired a child and overtly left room for error, however all attempts were unsuccessful. Accepting my fate, I gave up on the thought of having children. After failed relationships, an extended period of abstinence and a new found relationship, I found myself pregnant and in a very uncertain situation. I had to choose between my baby and her dad. Due to my upbringing and beliefs, I only had one option.

It was what I needed to do and my daughter is my greatest blessing. I admit that as time passed, I hope and prayed that he would come around and eventually change his stance and be involved but that was not the case. He was in no way giving in to me and I didn't see any other way. So be it, and so it was; just me and my baby. I found myself hurt and disappointed. It took a long time to get over it. Approximately 3 years and at times, I still have flashbacks like Madea, lol! I found a good Gospel CD that encouraged me beyond my pain; thanks Yolanda Adams! I had become a statistic; a single Mom with an absent father. Again, How? Why? I was my worst judge, constant condemnation.

I began to pick myself up, make the most of my pregnancy because I knew she would have a great Mother! I kept a camera in my purse and embraced it whole-heartedly with my head held high. You would have thought I had a super husband at home and my child was going to have a super Father! You see, I decided not to raise her with an absent father mentality, instead I vowed to raise her in a full–life mentality. I turned to God, repented and asked for forgiveness. I worked on forgiving myself. I appreciated my great and very supportive family. I then remembered that as a young girl, I went to the health department with a cousin and her baby.

As the receptionist called the patients, they all had names different than their children I thought I never want to be in that situation. I said a quiet prayer and never told anyone. Well, as I progressed in my pregnancy, I remembered my prayer. I often thought about what was not, but then I then realized that God had answered my simple childhood prayer by allowing me and my baby's Father to have the same last name. When he called to tell me that I would need him at the hospital, I told him, I didn't because my baby already had his last name, she just got it from a Man, my Father. Over the next years, I grew closer to God and worked on being the best mom I could be and the best person I could be. I started working on me and started learning to forgive others and myself. I began to develop my faith walk. I shifted from religion, that which was traditional, to Spirituality; that which is your personal relationship with God.

Journey 9/Day 1
Hurting, Healing, Forgiving
and Learning to Move Forward

Things will not change overnight; you continue to make mistakes. You start to make less and less and then you start having expectations. You stop worrying about what others expect from you. You learn from your mistakes and begin to live on a more conscious level. You become the driving force with a higher power in mind. You cease to exist and start living the life you are meant to live. I had to admit my mistakes, take note of the situation I created for myself and begin to mend some of the brokenness. In other words, I had to clean up my mess.

As the saying goes, its gets worse before it gets better. I was introduced to a "Man of God" and he was supposed to be the "Be all and End all." Not! He often said, "I don't want to be a liability." When what he really was saying that he was a liability, a casualty. The sad part for me was that I had an "Ah Ha" moment when we first met but didn't take heed. I heard what people had to say and got confused instead of doing what I knew to do: EXIT STAGE RIGHT! In other words, he may have been all they thought but it was really about what I thought and needed, not them. Instead, it was really a time that I was forced to stay on track, I almost got wrapped up but didn't. I found myself confused, but had to realize only Jesus saves, not me. Eventually finding that strength, I found courage to move out of that situation. There were positives in this relationship but enough was enough. I was done and I didn't need any more trials or tribulations. I needed triumphs not tragedies. A change was inevitable. A change was necessary and welcomed. After all, I was no longer going to be a victim or a statistic, instead a victor and a standard by which others would be measured. Some question it, but I totally embrace it. No longer bound, now I'm Saved, Single, and Satisfied!

Sometimes we allow the presumed picture to remain on display when we know it should have never been revealed. In short, deal with what is not what you or people want to believe. Make sure you are not tricked by Church folk or those you hold high. In short, the last relationship was with a minister, so it should have been perfect, right? Wrong, it was just another situation that I needed to go in with my eyes and ears open, never yielding to what other people thought. The thing that really made it bad, was that I begin to help cover up the issues and problems to help make it appear right. Confusion at its best! I also set out to prove people wrong, which was a big mistake. Sometimes you have to give up the right for the wrong! Growth! Instead of suffering in silence, I should have allowed my voice to be heard, my choice to be made and my greatness to be displayed! He was not my blessing, I was his!

It is said that the mind is a terrible thing to waste. In other words allow your thoughts to become your way of living. Change your thoughts and change your life! Allow your past to be the past! Today is a new day, embrace it! So from this point on you will draw a new blue print; renovate and renew you!

Choose a goal: set a personal goal regarding weight, work, relationship, education, living arrangements, travel, transportation, friends, life choices, etc? There must be a date set to start or stop something. It must be doable, obtainable, measurable, and observable. It can even be simple.

Reward: Decorate and accentuate the new you.

For example: Go out and get a make over, make under, mani-pedi, hair cut, wig, (the one you always wanted to try) a blackbald fade, grow a mustache (or not), Goat-T or Beard, buy a new dress, suit, shoes or take a 1-day trip. The goal is to go and do! Then come back and write, telling how you felt celebrating and rewarding yourself for putting you first!

Goal 1: (Set your own goal and write it here.)

_____

_____

_____

_____

_____

_____

_____

_____

_____

Reward: Learning to be good to self.

Journey 9/Day 1
Hurting, Healing, Forgiving and Learning to Move Forward

Goal 2: You will keep a calendar—timing is everything. Remember, time waits for no one! Time is of essence and should be valued; you never know when it's going to run out. You will move from your steal away moments to a "you day." You might choose to share it, "date night or family night" or not. Note the day and time has to be the same, the amount of time is up to you and depends on your circumstances.

Don't lock the children and husband out or forget to pick them up, just plan and make arrangements, it can and will be done!!!!

Reward: Uninterrupted 'You' time (spent only with you in mind).

Goal 3: Respect your progress, make note and prepare to move to I-live-here-drive. Yes, it's a gated community and Cul-de-sac. Only people with a need or who are welcome can visit. You now have the right to give out invitations—isn't that nice, it's your party and you are the guest of honor!

Reward: Prioritize people and things.

Goal 4: By now you have put things in perspective, place and even prioritized. You should find yourself with a desire to help someone or some cause. Volunteer and give back. This will be that reward that has no limit and will be life-long, helping you to fill your memory with new and positive memories because you survived all of the other ones.

Reward: Commit yourself to service and stick with it. There is such a great reward in giving and/or doing for someone you don't know and having a sense of purpose.

Please note: your goals and or reward may vary but must be adhered to.

(Note: When you heal, you move beyond you and look to help or be of service to others.)

During this journey, I have 3 small goals for you, you can do it, I have faith!

First, know that you are your brand, your best representative. So create your business card, even if it will only contain your personal contact information. You can't imagine how empowered you will feel when you hand them out. You can even go a step further and create your future business card, put it out there.

Secondly, purchase a dream/vision book and use it! Use for intended purposed only.

Habakkuk 2:2 says "And the Lord answered me, and said, write the vision and make it plain upon tables, that he may run that readeth it". I want you to start holding your self accountable. This should not include anything regarding work, church or family. This is personal, exclusively for you.

Lastly, identify something you have wanted to try that will incorporate you holistically: Mind, body and Spirit. Identify, sign up and do!

Reminder, tell someone about this, they will be your secret accountability partner and they will remind you without notice. When it comes up, you will probably be told how proud of you they are for what you have done, talk about a sense of accomplishment!

Journey 9/Day 2
Hurting, Healing, Forgiving and Learning to Move Forward

Write about a time when you were really hurt, directly or in-directly.

_____

_____

_____

_____

_____

_____

_____

_____

_____

_____

_____

_____

_____

_____

_____

_____

_____

_____

_____

_____

_____

Journey 9/Day 2
Hurting, Healing, Forgiving and Learning to Move Forward

Why do you think you hurt so bad? Was it the "who" or the "what?" Why do you think this happened to you? Who do or did you blame? As you journal make sure you allow yourself to be honest.

_____

_____

_____

_____

_____

_____

_____

_____

_____

_____

_____

_____

_____

_____

_____

_____

_____

_____

_____

_____

Journey 9/Day 3
Hurting, Healing, Forgiving and Learning to Move Forward

Write your favorite scripture or quote that represents healing. Write about why healing is important.

_____

_____

_____

_____

_____

_____

_____

_____

_____

_____

_____

_____

_____

_____

_____

_____

_____

_____

_____

_____

Journey 9/Day 4
Hurting, Healing, Forgiving and Learning to Move Forward

Write down some things that you have learned the hard way. Write down some lessons you wish you had skipped. Now write down something that may have had or continues to have a stronghold on you. This is something you can't seem to move from. Let's deal directly with that. The songwriter was correct when he said that you must hurt before you can heal. Peel away that Band-Aid and open that wound. Today we are treating it directly. Proper treatment equals proper healing.

_____

_____

_____

_____

_____

_____

_____

_____

_____

_____

_____

_____

_____

_____

_____

_____

_____

_____

Journey 9/Day 5
Hurting, Healing, Forgiving and Learning to Move Forward

Stand in the mirror and say to yourself, I forgive you over and over until you feel it and you mean it! Forgiveness is a gift of freedom waiting to be given. Release the hurt that you harbor for self or for love ones who you feel have wronged you. You deserve better!

_____

_____

_____

_____

_____

_____

_____

_____

_____

_____

_____

_____

_____

_____

_____

_____

_____

_____

_____

_____

Hurting, Healing, Forgiving and Learning to Move Forward

Challenge: Call, text, email or send a letter (think safety first) to someone that hurt you and tell them you forgive them for and mean it, let it go!

_____

_____

_____

_____

_____

_____

_____

_____

_____

_____

_____

_____

_____

_____

_____

_____

_____

_____

_____

_____

_____

_____

_____

Journey 9/Day 7

Hurting, Healing, Forgiving
and Learning to Move Forward

Reflection: How did it go this week? What worked, what didn't, and how did it all feel?

_____

_____

_____

_____

_____

_____

_____

_____

_____

_____

_____

_____

_____

_____

_____

_____

_____

_____

_____

_____

Prayer Changes Things (Your Mess Will become Your Message)

Some people meditate daily and some people pray without ceasing. The Bible speaks strongly about prayer. I am a believer that prayer changes things and prayer works! Be careful and make sure you truly understand the power of prayer.

I must say that I remember always hearing people say, "pray for me or keep me in your prayers." I remember people always telling other people, "I'm praying for you" but never really getting it.

Journey 10/Day 1

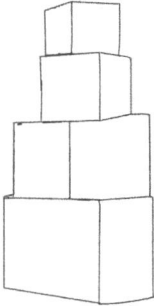

I was a very sad but seemingly happy teenager and young adult. I remember crying in high school when I thought no one was watching but my teachers at my new school were worried about me. I wasn't suicidal, but I think I had all the signs, they even secretly assigned a "Deana watch team," unbeknownst to me. I guess it was good but I didn't need it. By the time I got to college, I met new friends and had a blast, but I was still in so much pain. I would cry in between classes as I walked to and from the dorm or whenever I was alone. I would return home some weekends, go to church and testify. By the time I finished, it seemed like the whole church was crying. I would often say, "My name is Deana and this is my story." Boy did I have a story and a sad one too! I didn't mind telling it, I knew it word for word and recited it verbatim each time I told it. As I would leave church, I talked to the Pastor, Elder Watson, and he would say, "Pray about it daughter." I would always ask, "What is it?" I figured if he could tell me what "it" was, I could pray about "It" and pray "it" away.

I was so absorbed in my story. I had no song in my heart. I tried not to laugh because I surely thought it would be followed by sorrow. I was consumed in my own pity and victim mentality. But one day someone asked me about my Mom and her death and I had to think about it for the first time in my life and I realized "it" was gone. My prayers had been answered. I was no longer consumed by my story but now had a song in my heart. I finally had some Joy and Peace. What a revelation! You see I was praying and other people were praying and our prayers were answered. This gloom that had long overshadowed my life and me had been removed. The dawning of a new day was fast approaching on the horizon. "Weeping may endure for a night but joy comes in the morning." It is important to know that we are not talking about a 24-hour morning.

I also recall Mother's Day weekend in 1995, my sister, cousin and myself were traveling to my hometown and we got a call informing us that a car had hit my oldest nephew. Emotions were high, uncertainty was on board but I knew to begin praying. One of my cousins said to me, "I don't know why you are praying because God don't hear a sinner's prayer." I was troubled but I prayed anyway and prayed some more. He was in a coma for 11 days and was broken up, he was just a child. To make matters worse, the driver didn't even stop.

I put all that on the back burner because I had to get a prayer through. Later, I talked to one of the elder saints in my family and told her what my cousin had said. She went got the Bible and showed it to me. She said, "I don't know why she said that to you because she didn't tell you the whole verse. She pointed to it in the Bible and then to the comma just after that verse and it said, "Except Ye be sincere." WOW!!!! I am so glad I didn't listen but continued to pray and have faith. He woke up from his comma and started saying his alphabets backwards as I had taught him. Praise report! The Bible teaches that you should pray without ceasing and the effectual fervent prayers of the righteous availeth much! Remain steadfast and immovable always abounding in the work of the Lord!

Praise God! Our prayers were answered. Our baby Ray-Ray was going to be okay.

Journey 10/Day 1
Prayer Changes Things
(Your Mess will become Your Message)

Your prayer should be your conversation with God. It should reflect gratitude; your heart's desire and that His will be done. It should be much like a conversation and simple. No big words are needed, repentance is a must and faith is essential. Know that He is an On-time and Forgiving God!

DISCLAIMER

Note: Don't get caught up in word usage; rather get caught up in the work being done! If you don't pray; think, meditate, believe or whatever just do something, there is work to be done.

Journey 10/Day 1
Prayer Changes Things
(Your Mess will become Your Message)

Prayer is an invocation or act that seeks to activate a rapport with an object of worship through deliberate communication.

Meditation is a practice in which an individual trains the mind or induces a mode of consciousness.

Believe is to accept something as real or true.

Write about a time when you prayed (believed) for something major.

_____

_____

_____

_____

_____

_____

_____

_____

_____

_____

_____

_____

_____

_____

_____

_____

_____

_____

Journey 10/Day 2
Prayer Changes Things
(Your Mess will become your Message)

Remember how you felt when you knew your prayer/beliefs were answered, was the outcome what you wanted? Did you have to gain new perspective in order to understand what really happened?

Note: *Death is sometimes something that causes people to question their faith. But when one understands God, no question will arise!*

_____

_____

_____

_____

_____

_____

_____

_____

_____

_____

_____

_____

_____

_____

_____

_____

_____

_____

_____

_____

_____

Journey 10/Day 3
Prayer Changes Things
(Your Mess will become Your Message)

Write your favorite scripture or quote that talks about prayer or faith. What is important to you, prayer or faith? Do you believe that they are one in the same or vastly different? Can you have one and not the other? Write about a situation where your prayer or faith changed an outcome for you.

(For me it's God, for you it might be different but you must believe in something greater than self)

_____

_____

_____

_____

_____

_____

_____

_____

_____

_____

_____

_____

_____

_____

_____

_____

_____

_____

_____

Journey 10/Day 4
Prayer Changes Things
(Your Mess Will Become Your Message)

Visualize, draw or paste magazine images here to represent praying/meditating.

Journey 10/Day 5
Prayer Changes Things
(Your Mess will become your Message)

Take time out to pray and meditate consciously at the beginning and end of your day during this journey. It's OK to have a prayer partner; sometimes being held accountable helps you stay focused. At the end of the week, tell if you were consistent each day? Tell if things went better or remained the same.

_____

_____

_____

_____

_____

_____

_____

_____

_____

_____

_____

_____

_____

_____

_____

_____

_____

_____

_____

_____

Journey 10/Day 6
Prayer Changes Things
(Your Mess will become Your Message)

Go out and do something different to take your praying or meditation to a different level, find a different bible study group, prayer group, free yoga or pilates trial and just do it. Experience is priceless but moreso, if it is new or majorly different. If going out doesn't interest you, change your normal pattern, experience silence before you begin to pray and/or medidtate and increase your allotted time. Remember to come back and reflect on how you felt, emotionally and physically. Tell whether or not this came easy or if it was hard. Notice your distractions and try to decrease them.

_____

_____

_____

_____

_____

_____

_____

_____

_____

_____

_____

_____

_____

_____

_____

_____

_____

_____

Journey 10/Day 7
Prayer Changes Things
(Your Mess will Become your Message)

Reflection: How did it go this week? What worked, what didn't, and how did it all feel?

_____

_____

_____

_____

_____

_____

_____

_____

_____

_____

_____

_____

_____

_____

_____

_____

_____

_____

_____

_____

_____

Journey 11/Day 1
Finding Joy,
Letting go of Happy

Journey 11/Day 1

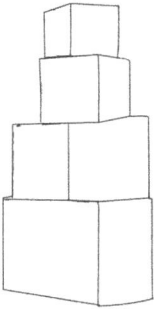

I once took a college philosophy class and I think I had the most radical teacher. My sister and cousin were both in that class and I know they would agree. He would come to class half dressed, used the most profane language, cause conflict and took debating to a whole new level. He challenged you beyond measure and sought to disturb your mental being. He would trample over your psyche and eat your morals for lunch. Students would report him to administration, their parents and or anyone who would listen. That never stopped him; he would feed off of the attention and dare to go further the next class. There were no topics off limits and no topics that he wouldn't speak his mind on.

There were several things that I took got from his class that I used in my life that made a difference.

First, know that Happy is not a true state of being. It is instead, the result of something. If good things happen, you're happy. If bad things happen, you're unhappy, this is not Joy. In other words, Happy is conditional and Joy is unconditional.

Secondly, never let anyone move you out of who you are. In other words, you can be angry, upset and bothered but never let anyone move you out of who you truly are. If someone can move you, they have control over you.

Lastly, opinions are like lives, everyone has one!

So I invite you to seek Joy. Joy is a gift from God. It gives you peace in the midst of the storm. It is that peace that surpasses all understanding. It allows you to go through your storms and remain steadfast and immovable. It acknowledges that although you have freedom of choice you are not in control. It gives you comfort even when God allows it to rain in your life. It allows you to have a "not yet" praise and praise on the inside that you can't keep to yourself.

Joy doesn't erase the pain, hurt, sorrow, or tears. It's just a comfort in knowing, IGBOK (it's going to be OK). You know that there is nothing too hard for God. You know that the battle is not yours. You learn to be still. In joy you become slow to anger. You learn to respond and not react! There is newness in an old
you. Joy makes the best of what is out of what was. You realize the true place of peace.

You become the Thermostat and not a thermometer! In other words, you set the temperature, you don't just measure it!

Journey 11/Day 1
Finding Joy, Letting go of Happy

It is cliché' to say one person's trash is another person's treasure. Well, I once heard it said that even in the trash, there once was treasure. So sometimes you have to sift through and reflect to find truth. Once you have truth, you can begin to MOVE. Let's begin to grow here. Let's begin to Get M.O.V.E.D. (mapping out victory each day) from this point on. Let's start by letting go of happy and finding JOY! You know the Joy that the world didn't give to you and the world can't take it away!

Trash Revisited:
Being once foolish, made me wise.

Being weak helped me to realize my strength.

Seeking and finding Joy gave me Peace.

Realizing I was out of control, made me seek who was in Control.

For example: The liar made me know that honesty is a must, the cheater made me know that faithfulness and loyalty are a must. Inconsistency made me realize consistency mattered. The immature made me mature and seek maturity, the lack of made me appreciate what I did have; enemies made me appreciate my friends; getting fired made me be a better worker; humiliation made me humble, being belittled and demeaned made me recognize my value and worth; being mistreated made me stand up for me; silence evokes voice and pain made me seek out love.

What are your examples?

_____

_____

_____

_____

_____

Journey 11/Day 2
Finding Joy, Letting go of Happy

Write about a time when something that once brought you happiness, later brought you sadness.

_____

_____

_____

_____

_____

_____

_____

_____

_____

_____

_____

_____

_____

_____

_____

_____

_____

_____

_____

_____

_____

_____

_____

_____

_____

Finding Joy, Letting go of Happy

How did you get over it? How did you move on? Do you know how to speak life? Do you know that if you change your words, you change your thoughts? Do you know that if you change your mind, you change your heart?

_____

_____

_____

_____

_____

_____

_____

_____

_____

_____

_____

_____

_____

_____

_____

_____

_____

_____

_____

_____

_____

Journey 11/Day 3
Finding Joy, Letting go of Happy

Now that you know yourself on a deeper and more intimate level, what brings you joy?

_____

_____

_____

_____

_____

_____

_____

_____

_____

_____

_____

_____

_____

_____

_____

_____

_____

_____

_____

Journey 11/Day 4
Finding Joy, Letting go of Happy

What is your greatest treasure?

_____

_____

_____

_____

_____

_____

_____

_____

_____

_____

_____

_____

_____

_____

_____

_____

_____

_____

_____

_____

Journey 11/Day 5
Finding Joy, Letting go of Happy

Go out and do something that will bring joy to someone else! Write about how they reacted. Write about how that made your feel.

_____

_____

_____

_____

_____

_____

_____

_____

_____

_____

_____

_____

_____

_____

_____

_____

_____

_____

_____

_____

_____

_____

_____

_____

Journey 11/Day 6
Finding Joy, Letting go of Happy

This challenge will be different, check your local forecast. On various days, go out and allow yourself to feel and experience the gifts of rain, sun, wind and humidity. Experience raindrops, bathe in the sun, feel the wind on your face, and allow the humidity to make you a little uncomfortable. Gaze at the sunset, the stars, or try to catch the sun rising. In other words, breathe the breath of life by acknowledging life. Now write about it.

_____

_____

_____

_____

_____

_____

_____

_____

_____

_____

_____

_____

_____

_____

_____

_____

_____

_____

_____

Journey 11/Day 7
Finding Joy, Letting go of Happy

Reflection: How did it go this week? What worked, what didn't, and how did it all feel?

_____

_____

_____

_____

_____

_____

_____

_____

_____

_____

_____

_____

_____

_____

_____

_____

_____

_____

_____

_____

_____

_____

_____

Living and not existing:

Existing is just doing. Living is consciously doing.

For many years, I thought I was living because I was not exhibiting the signs of depression or death. I would do what I had to do, what others needed me to do and just do busy work in between. Never realizing that I lost myself somewhere along the way. I even became a Mother, friend, mate and support system to many. I was having a conversation with a family member about how she once got off drugs with no rehab and she told me she asked God to remove the desires from her heart because she was tired of just existing and not living.

Journey 12/Day 1

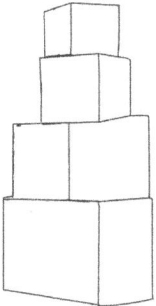

I thought how sad she must have been. Then I started looking at my life. Was I not doing the same after all was said and done? I got up and went to work because it was morning. I went to sleep because it was nighttime. In between, I did whatever I was supposed to do. I existed. I was not living my life. My life was what everyone one else needed it to be, convenient and available. I realized I had dreams, goals and aspirations that I had left behind in the dust. I was created with a Purpose. I realized that I didn't do anything that was simply for me; I was selfless. My life had no balance and very little me.

I had to check myself. I had to learn what not to do and what I needed to do. I had to yield myself to my Purpose. I had to Live and not die. I had to cease existing and actively participate in life. I had to learn and exemplify loving self before loving others. I had to respect what I had been given and not take it for granted or lightly. I had to yield to my higher power, GOD!

Journey 12/Day 1
Living and not existing:

Finally...

- I began to get to know me on a personal, professional, and holistic level.

- I looked back at my goals and put them back into play, and then I went after them with a mission.

- I set new goals and started removing what I was taught; I begin to rise above the walls of fear that I previously misinterpreted as being cautious. My fear of failure had led me to now having a fear of success.

- I accepted my purpose without hesitation and I began to keep it on the forefront!

- I removed my tunnel vision and opened my eyes to broader horizons!

- I removed the limitations that were placed on me or placed by me because greatness is in me!

- I believe and now know that greater and bigger things await me!

- I live life with open eyes, an open mind, and an open heart!

- I began to let my light shine and strive daily to let Him direct my path!

- I set new goals and will from now on; if you don't keep moving you will become stagnant!

- Lastly, I know Who is in control and I know that what God has for me, it is for me!

Journey 12/Day 1
Living and not existing:

Write about a time when you purposely completed something. How did you feel? Write about when you had no reason to move. What caused you to not? Map out your accomplishments on the timeline provided on page 142. This is not pass or fail, good or bad, instead it should be enlightening.

_____

_____

_____

_____

_____

_____

_____

_____

_____

_____

_____

_____

_____

_____

_____

_____

_____

_____

_____

_____

_____

_____

_____

_____

Journey 12/Day 2
Prepare to be moved.

Here is real reflection of my timeline. This was a real eye opener for me. There was such a big gap between 2002 and 2015, WOW! As you can see, I have already set goal/aspirations for the next year. No more existing for me, from now on I choose to LIVE!! Please note that whatever your timeline reveals to you, consider it an opportunity for betterment/change. Prepare for success.

SUCCESS IS WHERE PREPARATION AND OPPORTUNITY MEET! Welcome to your next!
Remember, the difference between a dream and a goal is that a goal has a date! You must plan, strategize and work! Faith without works is dead!

This is not a one shot deal, this is an ongoing process. In short, a lifestyle change!

WRITE THE VISION AND MAKE IT PLAIN!

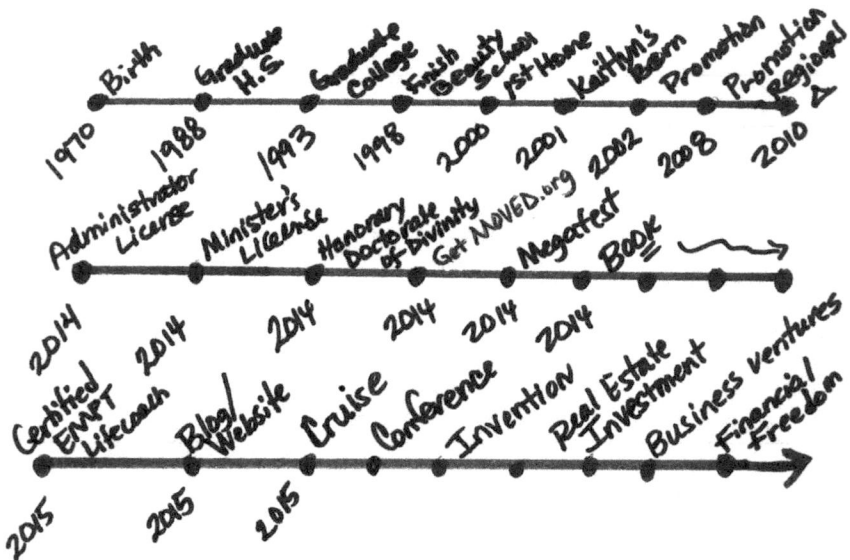

Journey 12/Day 2
Living and not existing:

What does your timeline reveal about your life? Have you been busy, productive or stagnant?

_____

_____

_____

_____

_____

_____

_____

_____

Mark your time line here, what will it reveal about you?

_____

_____

Journey 12/Day 3
Living and not existing:

Your goal is to be victorious, read a scripture or find a quote that talks about VICTORY. Now write about it!

_____

_____

_____

_____

_____

_____

_____

_____

_____

_____

_____

_____

_____

_____

_____

_____

_____

_____

_____

_____

_____

_____

_____

_____

_____

_____

_____

_____

Journey 12/Day 4
Living and not existing:

Visualize, draw or paste magazine images here to represent victory, winning and/or determination

Journey 12/Day 5
Living and not existing:

Go out and celebrate your recent accomplishments, make sure you dress up.

_____

_____

_____

_____

_____

_____

_____

_____

_____

_____

_____

_____

_____

_____

_____

_____

_____

_____

_____

_____

_____

_____

_____

_____

Journey 12/Day 6
Living and not existing:

Go out and do something that used to frighten you, because now you are empowered! Fear not, You can do anything! Now write about it!

_____

_____

_____

_____

_____

_____

_____

_____

_____

_____

_____

_____

_____

_____

_____

_____

_____

_____

_____

_____

_____

_____

_____

_____

Journey 12/Day 7
Living and not existing:

Reflection: how did it go this week? What worked, what didn't, and how did it all feel?

_____

_____

_____

_____

_____

_____

_____

_____

_____

_____

_____

_____

_____

_____

_____

_____

_____

_____

_____

_____

_____

_____

_____

Afterthought before you go

Remember, this book should serve as a resource, not a one-time read. It should be a reflection of your progress. The cliché say that Home is where the heart is! I hope this can be home base.

Home is essential. It is a place of comfort and refuge. It offers protection, shelter and safety. Although your living arrangements may vary, you need a place to call home, be it a book or a tool. So, here is your tool. I hope you incorporate these things in your life as core values to help you in times of trouble. I have used keys from a keyboard or telephone for symbolic representation: Use these keys as you move forth in life.

Home row: your safe haven, your comfort zone, where you retreat if need be.

Enter: validate your action.

Send: set things in motion. Do with purpose, not by accident.

End: knowing things have run their course, don't just linger and hold on

Delete: some things should be deleted, no longer in your presence or existence. Remove the temptation.

Password protected: own it. Keep some things sacred and personal.

Function: is it serving your purpose?

Control: you are empowered to be in control. Operate in your authority.

Shift: know when change is necessary.

Alt/control: sometimes you have to rely on a higher power.

Backspace: mistakes are an opportunity for making necessary corrections.

Escape: closure or an alternate route.

Power: the choice to start, stop, resume, or Get M.O.V.E.D.

What will be your first 3 keys?

1. _____

2. _____

3. _____

(My 1st key was delete. I had old friends, deceased family members, old boyfriends, etc; I had to let go!)

Afterthought before you go

I have to share: I have a family Member, Bea, and one day I heard her say that if people didn't answer her call, she would delete their number because if they didn't have time to answer she didn't have time to call. Later, I heard a man say, "After all is said and done, there is more said than done!" Well, I try to always do a self-check and it was time. I had a dear friend who wasn't answering my calls and picked up whenever they felt like it. I decided to do more and say less, by deleting that contact. It felt satisfying and empowering. Delete became my new friend. In other words, when you come to a certain level of empowerment and conscious living, accepting anything less than what you deserve; casualties will increase which makes your inner circle decrease. Remember, dead things need to be buried! Stop giving CPR to dead situations!

EMPOWERMENT IS EMPOWERING!!!!!
Now that you have been M.O.V.E.D., draw or paste your new picture here.
(Hint: It's beautiful and it's not retouched or photo-shopped!)

Afterthought before you go con't.

I didn't want your picture side by side because there is always a beginning and end. When you place them side-by-side it seems too easy. Leave it to the imagination. This way you know that it may have not been easy, pretty or kind, but you did it! You will see a change in you that others will want to know how you did it, what you did and how can they do it. Go ahead, help them MOVE, your purpose will just keep enlarging its territory. Your storyline has become your glory line. (All honor, praise and glory belong to God!) Hello to the new you! MOVED and IMPROVED!

Now that you have been M.O.V.E.D, you will unconsciously Map Out (Your) Victory Each Day!!!! (Without much effort)

So, you know me...You should be able to VERIFY!

So, I give you the 6-P check-up.

Your thoughts on pain, perspective, perception, priorities, praise, and prance should be DIFFERENT!

Certainty:
Every problem has a solution, every question an answer, every action a reaction, every day a night (seen or not seen), every story has two sides and every birth has a death?

Correct-a –Mondo!!!!!!!!!!!!!!

Therefore, I feel that you should not have to take my word that you have been changed; instead you should be able to make me and others know how you have been change. No explanation needed but what a great thing to know yourself enough to enlighten others in your growth! What an AWESOME AND WONDERFUL FEELING to EXPERIENCE.

I am so proud of you!!!!!!
We have journeyed for 12 wks!
Welcome to your new season!
You are Empowered!

Acknowledgements

To my sisters: Mary the epitome of strength, Melinda the epitome of wisdom and Patricia the epitome of unconditional love. My brothers: Doray, my constant help and Michael the my dose of laughter, you all make me who I am. There would be no me without y'all! I could go on and on but there is nothing like our relationship. Yes we are human, yes we fuss and disagree but we share a bond that many will never experience and what seems unimaginable to some.

To my sisters and brothers from my other Mothers, Lowanna, Lourey, Melvin, and Deon, a huge thank you for sharing and extending your love. Thank each and every one for your acceptance of me; the good and the bad and your unconditional love. Thanks for seeing me at my worse and accepting me for who I was. Thanks for loving me. To my in-laws that were outlaws from time to time, I am eternally grateful for all of your love & support.

To my extended family: nieces and nephews, aunts, uncles and cousins, from infinity to infinity you were where the reason I made it. Each one of you played a key role in my every footstep.

Thank you Lubertha Jackson (Bea) for opening your doors and lives up to us from day one when it seemed everything was impossible. Mary North-Thompson, what can I say as thank you doesn't seem enough? Thanks for showing me what humility really is. Mrs. Shirlene Foster and Ms. Juasita Seaton thank you for noticing me and not letting go. Tommie Flowers-Davis, encore! You heard my cry and provided the highway and bi-way. Sheila, thanks for keeping it real at all times! To Mane, Marvin and LC, the three that will always be my favorite uncles, thanks for everything!!!!!!!!!!!!

To my cousin Seth, thanks for never allowing me to stop. Keith and Tracey, thanks for all of your love and encouragement.

To my greatest blessing, Kaitlyn, thank you for inspiring me. Thank you for giving me another reason to live and not exist. You make me a better me. Thank you for loving me not because I am mom but because you want to. You evoke a joy in me and quicken the spirit of my soul. I love sharing belly-filled laughter with you; the laughter that involves your soul and makes your body shake. As a little girl, this was that "thing" I loved to see my mom experience. It is so nice to share that with you because laughter is the cushion to life's disappointments. I only hope and pray that you share this simple thing with your generations to come. To the love of my life God, thank you! For not making me a statistic, instead a survivor!

To my friends/cousins: Ann, Eunice, Kathy, Bonita, Bora, Pat, and Sheila I can never ever give to you what y'all have given me. I am eternally grateful. Special thanks to Tia for not only pushing me but standing in the gap for me. To my Brother Spud and my nephews Kyran, Devon and Andre who have transitioned, RIL and RIP. Cynt, may you continue to RIL, thanks for showing me what true unconditional love was and how to give and receive it. To the best staff ever, Chenal Therapy Department, (Kathy, Keshia, Connie, Chess, Casey, Greg, Marcella, Audrey, Sally, Gloria, Mallory, and DeOdis) I have grown because of each of you! Thanks to all of the T-Th Dance Moms at Tidwell's Centre for the DansArts, for your love, support, surveys and pick-ups/drop-offs, you guys rock!

Special thanks to Chenal Rehab, the patients and staff, somewhere you contributed to my growth and development daily! To the greatest Pastor, Pastor Michael Perkins and 1st Lady Gloria Perkins and the New Hope Church Family!

www.ingramcontent.com/pod-product-compliance
Lightning Source LLC
Chambersburg PA
CBHW072012090426
42740CB00011B/2159